JOHN AND CHARLES WESLEY

JOHN AND CHARLES WESLEY

Selected Prayers, Hymns, and Sermons

Foreword by Peter J. Gomes

Introduction by Frank Whaling

Edited by Emilie Griffin

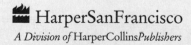
HarperSanFrancisco
A Division of HarperCollins*Publishers*

JOHN AND CHARLES WESLEY: *Selected Prayers, Hymns, and Sermons.* Original translation published by Paulist Press, 997 Macarthur Boulevard, Mahwah, NJ 07430; www.paulistpress.com. Copyright © 1981 by the Missionary Society of St. Paul the Apostle in the State of New York. Foreword © 2004 by Peter J. Gomes. All rights reserved. Printed in the United States of America. No part of this book may be used or reproduced in any matter whatsoever without written permission except in the case of brief quotations embodied in critical articles and reviews. For information address HarperCollins Publishers, Inc., 10 East 53rd Street, New York, NY 10022.

HarperCollins books may be purchased for educational, business, or sales promotional use. For information please write: Special Markets Department, HarperCollins Publishers, Inc., 10 East 53rd Street, New York, NY 10022.
HarperCollins Web site: http://www.harpercollins.com
HarperCollins®, ■®, and HarperSanFrancisco™ are trademarks of HarperCollins Publishers, Inc.

Book Design by Susan Rimerman

FIRST EDITION

Library of Congress Cataloging-in-Publication Data is available upon request.

ISBN 0–06–0576510
04 05 06 07 08 RRD(H) 10 9 8 7 6 5 4 3 2 1

CONTENTS

FOREWORD

Although brought up in the Christian church and in a believing household, it is fair to say that I first came to a personal knowledge of the Christian faith through the experience of the hymns of the church, and that none were more effectual in shaping my religious sensibility than the hymns of Charles and John Wesley. Nearer than scripture, more accessible than theology, the hymns—especially the Wesleyans'—of the church in which I was raised provided me a vocabulary with which to sing about that which I did not yet understand. I am convinced that, should I be sentient at death's door, the last words on my lips will not be those of scripture or creedal formulation but the half-remembered words of some hymn deeply engraved upon my heart, and that those words will be the last I leave as I leave this world.

If it is somewhat heretical for a preacher to concede that hymnody is more important than theology in the shaping of belief and experience, I confess that I was a church musician before I was a minister. This office I inherited from my mother, a Baptist preacher's daughter and a conservatory-trained organist, singer, and choir trainer. Through playing the piano in Sunday School, then at evening service, and eventually on Sunday morning, I learned both the music and the words of the church's sons and daughters, and thus came my discovery that many of the most effective were written by the Wesley brothers.

While a divinity student at Harvard, I did field work as organist of the Memorial Methodist Church in Plymouth, Massachusetts, where the congregation consisted largely of the descendants of English wool workers, Methodists who kept alive the musical tradition of Wesleyan Methodism; and although Methodist theology and polity eluded me, Methodist hymnody and the piety it represented became mine by adoption and grace. John Wesley famously said, "I look upon all the world as my parish," and all of us in the Christian world are his grateful parishioners. In saying, however, "Once in seven years I burn all my sermons, for it is a shame if I cannot write better sermons now than I did seven years ago," he set a terrifying example for all preachers who are apt to be seduced by their own preaching. It is to John Wesley that I turn when I aspire to a rule of life, rather than to Benjamin Franklin, George Washington, or even Lord Chesterton, each famous for producing such codes. In a letter, John Wesley wrote:

> Do all the good you can,
> By all the means you can,
> In all the ways you can,
> In all the places you can,
> At all the times you can,
> To all the people you can,
> As long as ever you can.

For what it means to sing the praises of the Christian faith, though, it is to John's brother Charles that I, along with many millions of others, turn. Charles Wesley has given us the definitive hymn of Easter, almost universally sung on Easter day:

Christ the Lord is risen today, Alleluia!
Sons of men and angels say; Alleluia!
Raise your joys and triumphs high; Alleluia!
Sing, ye heavens, thou earth reply. Alleluia!

He wrote this hymn in 1739, and it is in every hymnal in the Christian world. Charles also wrote that hymn of almost embarrassing intimacy, "Jesus, lover of my soul/Let me to thy bosom fly"; and as if to demonstrate that the Christian faith was as militant as it was pious, he wrote:

Soldiers of Christ, arise, and put your armour on;
Strong in the strength that God supplies through
his eternal Son: Strong in the Lord of hosts, and
in his mighty power;
Who in the strength of Jesus trusts is more than
conqueror.

At Advent, Charles Wesley has the whole church sing:

Lo! He comes with clouds descending,
Once for favoured sinners slain;
Thousand thousand saints attending
Swell the triumph of his train: Alleluia!

He has given us the most familiar and beloved Christmas hymn:

Hark! The herald angels sing
Glory to the new-born king,

> Peace on earth, and mercy mild,
> God and sinners reconciled.

Perhaps the finest hymn in all of Christendom, and the most sublime summary of the faith that moves countless hearts and minds, is Charles Wesley's:

> Love divine, all loves excelling,
> Joy of heaven, to earth come down;
> Fix in us thy humble dwelling,
> All thy faithful mercies crown.
> Jesu, thou art all compassion,
> Pure, unbounded love thou art;
> Visit us with thy salvation,
> Enter every trembling heart.

The theme of the love of God is not alien to Christian hymnody, and many lyricists have attempted to translate into song the great words of St. Paul in I Corinthians, chapter 13. Few have achieved that ambition so memorably as Charles Wesley, for whom love is the work of a continuing and renewed creation which leads only to that consummation and bliss that is the end of all Christian striving. He says, in the final verses:

> Finish then thy new creation,
> Pure and spotless let us be;
> Let us see thy great salvation
> Perfectly restored in thee;
> Changed from glory into glory,

Till in heaven we take our place,
Till we cast our crowns before thee,
Lost in wonder, love, and praise.

To look into the index of composers in any Christian hymnal in the world is to find that the name of Charles Wesley leads them in quantity as well as in the quality of poetic theological reflection. In his hymn "O, for a thousand tongues to sing," we see Charles Wesley's gift to those who both think and sing:

He speaks, and listening to his voice,
New life the dead receive;
The mournful broken hearts rejoice;
The humble poor believe.

In an age when Christians across the world—even, alas, the peculiar people called Methodists—are increasingly known by that which divides them, the inheritance of John and Charles Wesley continues to enrich the whole community of faith. When we need to borrow language to express the inexpressible hopes and joys of the faithful heart we will, for centuries yet to come and until we join the heavenly choir, turn to the inexhaustible treasure of the Wesleys, for theirs is a school of prayer, praise, and song for a world ever new, ever renewing.

—PETER J. GOMES, D.D.

INTRODUCTION

John and Charles Wesley were two of the greatest Christians of the modern age of the church. Charles Wesley is famous as probably the finest hymn writer in Christian history, and this volume includes forty of his hymns, which convey a distinctive spirituality. John Wesley's spiritual experience, sometimes compared to that of St. Augustine and Martin Luther, led him to become a great Christian leader and the founder of the Methodist tradition.

The Wesleys transformed the spiritual atmosphere of Britain in the eighteenth century, and they paved the way for the rise of a present-day Methodist community of almost fifty million around the world. But the influence of their spirituality cannot be confined to that community. They combined a concern for organization and inwardness, fellowship and the individual, the social and the spiritual, sacrament and evangelism, theology and practice, body and soul, life present and life to come, spiritual seriousness and spiritual gaiety, and liturgy and spontaneity. Contemporary Methodists and all Christian believers have much to learn from the integrity and the integralism of the Wesleys' spirituality.

It is appropriate that the Wesleys should be considered together. They not only shared the youthful fellowship of the family environment of Epworth Rectory in Lincolnshire, but also attended the same Oxford college, Christ Church; they shared the life of the same Holy Club at Oxford. They went out to Georgia together, and they shared a similar spiritual experience in 1738 after their disappointment in Georgia. Their mutual aim was that of perfect love for God and humankind. They retained their joint love for the Church of England while leading the Methodist revival, and their spirituality was similar and also complementary.

It would be wrong, of course, to assume that the Wesleys were carbon copies of each other. This was far from the case. Of the two, John was the more natural leader and organizer; his mind was more wide-ranging than Charles's. But in spite of the excellence of John's early translations of German pietist hymns, it was Charles who had the greater poetic gifts. It is also clear that Charles exercised his spirituality within the parameters of a happy family life with his wife and children, whereas John's attempts at nuptials were little short of disastrous. His failure to marry Sophia Hopkey in Georgia triggered a series of events leading to the court case that caused him to leave America. Later he did not marry Grace Murray, who would have shared his preaching as well as his love. Finally he did marry a widow, Mrs. Vazeille, who was an unsuitable partner. John's spirituality became essentially that of the traveling preacher; Charles's became that of the more sedentary spiritual leader in Bristol and later in London. However, in spite of these differences, it is remarkable how close the Wesley brothers were in their basic spirituality.

John Wesley was born at Epworth in 1703 into a family that could already boast two generations of ministers. His parents were both strong-minded people who were Church of England by conviction, in contrast with Wesley's grandparents, who had been Dissenters by conviction. His family had a deep influence on John Wesley, and also on his brother Charles, who was born four years later, in 1707. Their mother, Susanna Wesley, was a woman of very strong character who ruled the children through a benevolent despotism that involved "breaking their wills" by the time they were age one.

When John barely survived a fire at the rectory at the age of seven, Susanna had an intuition that he was destined for great things, and she spared no effort to aid his spiritual development. By her weekly private conferences, her letters, her advocacy of spiritual masters such as Pascal, her religious instruction in the Apostles' Creed and the Ten Commandments, and her own personal example, she fueled the mind and imagination of her son. From his father, John learned to value the sacraments, to take seriously the Protestant and Roman Catholic mystics, to distrust Calvinistic particularism, to be assiduous in the work of the ministry, to value the fellowship to be found through the Church of England societies, and not least, to cherish inward religion. The elements of Wesley's later spirituality were already there in germ in the rectory at Epworth.

John Wesley entered Christ Church at Oxford University in 1720 and was elected to a fellowship at Lincoln College in 1726, the same year that Charles enrolled at Christ Church. Oxford was significant for John in a number of ways. At the practical level it gave him a base of operations; in that Oxford fellowship he could preach without having a parish. Oxford enabled Wesley to train his keen intellect and to build up his formidable mind. Throughout his life, he was to retain a curiosity about many divergent subjects, and in later years he would continue to investigate new areas of thought. To these he brought a logical, reasoning mind that was sharpened at Oxford by his teaching of Greek and philosophy, and above all by his (at one stage) daily leading of disputations among the undergraduates. This enabled him to pierce quickly to the heart of a complicated sequence of thoughts, a habit that would remain with him.

The secret of his wide-ranging spirituality lay in the fact that he was a "Methodist," methodical in his use of time, so that interiority, preaching, reading, writing, and organizing were attended to in their due order within his overarching purpose of loving and communing with God in all that he did. For Wesley Christianity was not primarily a set of beliefs; it was an experimental way, a process, an inwardness based on orthodox doctrines and resulting in outward practice. Accordingly, his main theological concern was for those doctrines most directly concerned with experiential Christianity, namely, prevenient grace, justification by faith, assurance, sanctification, and perfect love. He used his formidable powers of reason to commend experiential Christianity and those doctrines most fitted to apply it within the lives of ordinary men and women.

Wesley's interest in writings on mysticism and interiority continued throughout his stay in Oxford and indeed beyond it. His Oxford interest in mysticism extended to include non-British and non–Church of England writers, including the Roman Catholics Pascal, Scupoli, Quesnel, Fénelon, de Renty, Mme. Bourignon, Mme. Guyon, Tauler, the *Theologica Germanica*, and Molinos, with their emphasis upon pure love and total resignation. His later contact with the Moravians made him react for a time against the mystics, but he later reacted against the Moravians themselves, who took faith and fellowship seriously, but who were less concerned with the requirements of the means of grace and even outward works in their zeal for inward mystical faith. However, the notion that Wesley suddenly repudiated the mystical influences on his development and abandoned them forever is an erroneous one. He assimilated the things that were helpful to him, and to the movement that grew up as a result of his work, from any and every source. The fifty volumes of his *Christian Library* of 1750–56 include the works of five French and three Spanish Roman Catholic mystics, namely, Pascal, Brother Lawrence, Fénelon, Mme. Guyon, Mme. Bourignon, John of Avila, Lopez, and Molinos.

At Oxford, Wesley also gained much from his leadership of the Holy Club. This group of students had formed around Charles Wesley to engage in Bible study, systematic devotions, and regular Communion—and to investigate studiously and analyze the implications of the works of the fourth-century monastic fathers and the liturgical practices of the early church. After John's return to Oxford in 1729 he assumed leadership of this group. Vulgar nicknames were given to this serious-minded fellowship of people who were keen about religious practices. The one that stuck was the name "Methodist."

It was in the Methodist environment of the Holy Club that Wesley learned to be methodical not just in his study of the Bible, but in the discipline of his whole life. The secret of his spirituality lay in his careful and prayerful use of time. It was his methodical habits consecrated to God that later enabled him to accomplish so much. Within the Holy Club he led a disciplined personal life, visited the prisoners in Oxford gaol, showed concern for the debtors, helped start a school, went to the relief of the poor, discovered he could live on twenty-eight pounds a year, and maintained a high-church stance in regard to the sacraments, the fasts of the church, confession, penance, and mortification.

The Holy Club set Wesley's search for and study of holiness within a social context. For him spirituality, though inward, was not a solitary thing. He felt that fellowship was vital to Christian spirituality and that there was no such thing as a solitary Christian.

Wesley had learned much from the Holy Club, but he was not fated to remain in Oxford, nor to succeed his father at Epworth after his father's death in 1735. Instead, as the opportunity arose for the Holy Club to move its sphere of activities to Georgia, Charles and John Wesley took ship for America to missionize the Indians and the Georgian colonists. George Whitefield of the Holy Club promised to follow after ordination. The bare facts of John's Georgian expedition are printed in the records of the colony: "Minister at Savannah; embark'd 14 Oct. 1735; arrived Feb. 1735–6; run away 3 Dec. 1737."[1] They appear to constitute a debacle. Apparently his Enlightenment view of the Indians as "noble savages" was not borne out, some of his high-church principles were unsuitable to the local context, and his amorous entanglement with Sophia Hopkey resulted in impending legal action.

[1] E. M. Coulter and A. B. Saye, eds., *A List of Early Settlers of Georgia* (Athens, GA, 1949), p. 57.

In reality, however, those years represent a period of bewilderment and spiritual seeking during which he was able to explore more fully his own self and the will of God for his life. It was in Georgia that he began to condense a number of mystical works and began the theological work on the Old and New Testaments that would bear fruit later. In Georgia he experimented with some of the features of his later organization, including societies, bands, lay leaders, extempore prayer and preaching, love feasts, and chapel buildings, and it was there also that he learned German and beautifully translated a number of German hymns.

The trauma of the flight from Georgia had heightened Wesley's desire to experience inwardly a sense of trust and confidence in God. Both he and Charles, who had also returned bewildered from Georgia, needed some relief from their inner and outer uncertainty, some resolution concerning the future direction of their outward lives. They needed to ascertain the will of God for them. Moravian Peter Böhler convinced Wesley that inward peace was graspable. He produced witnesses to persuade Wesley that it was possible to experience an inner assurance of faith. His brother, Charles, realized this experience on May 21, 1738. On May 24, John opened his New Testament at the words of 2 Peter 1:4: "There are given unto us exceeding great and precious promises, even that ye should be partakers of the divine nature." The afternoon anthem at St. Paul's was "Out of the depths have I cried unto thee, O Lord" (Ps. 130). In the evening he went "unwillingly" to a society in Aldersgate Street, where someone was reading Luther's preface to the letter to the Romans. His journal summarizes succinctly and brilliantly what happened:

"About a quarter before nine, while he was describing the change which God works in the heart through faith in Christ, I felt my heart strangely warmed. I felt I did trust in Christ, Christ alone for salvation; and an assurance was given me that he had taken away my sins, even mine, and saved me from the law of sin and death."

The year 1739 represents a watershed in the development of Wesley's spirituality. Up to this time, he had been learning from others. From now on, although he continued to learn, others would be far more influenced by him. In 1725 he had heard the call to a deeper spiritual life. In 1729 he had led a band of Oxford men who together, in sheltered circumstances, sought after perfect love. In 1735 he had gone into the wilderness—almost literally in Georgia, symbolically in his soul—to ascertain God's will for the future and to do some good in the present. And in 1738–39 he discovered an inner dynamic that fused together the other elements in his interior life and an outward role that would enable him to convey his own spirituality to others. The rest of his life was basically the story of how Wesley endeavored under God to communicate his personal spirituality to countless thousands of others.

The development of Charles Wesley's spirituality followed the general course taken by his brother's. Charles had become a student, then a lecturer at Christ Church, Oxford, and the first leader of the Holy Club before the return of his brother in 1729. They had both gone out to Georgia, John to Savannah, and Charles to be secretary to Oglethorpe, the leading spirit in the new plantation. Charles quit Georgia before John, in July 1736, and he arrived home without any resolution of his inner spiritual need for a personal assurance of faith and of his vocational need for a set direction for his ministry. On May 21, 1738, three days before his brother, he received an inward assurance of faith. Influenced by Luther's commentary on Galatians, he heard an inward voice asking him to arise and believe, and through the medium of interior words such as these and Scripture passages such as Isaiah 40:1 ("Comfort ye, comfort ye my people, says your God"), he found a new inner dynamic.

He also found a new vocation, for he felt compelled to put his experience into the words of a hymn that begins "Where shall my wondering soul begin?" Although famous, it is not one of the best of his hymns. Nor, indeed, was it the first. Yet it pointed to a latent gift for hymnody. Like John, he was destined to preach, undergo persecution, organize, and travel in the course of his work, but the main thrust of his spirituality lay in the hymns that now began to pour from his pen.

What then was the religious stage onto which the Wesleys were about to enter with dynamic force? New towns were growing up in the north of England largely bereft of spiritual sustenance. At the beginning of the eighteenth century, Manchester had eight thousand inhabitants; by the end of the century it would have ninety-five thousand people within its boundaries. Churches and ministers were not present to meet the growing needs. And it was upon this stage that the Wesley brothers lit England, and later America, on fire for God and the gospel.

—FRANK WHALING

Adapted from the Introduction to *John and Charles Wesley: Selected Writings and Hymns* (Paulist Press, 1981).

SELECTED WRITINGS OF JOHN WESLEY

John Wesley's Spirituality: A Collection of Forms of Prayer for Every Day in the Week

First printed in 1733

Preface

The intention of the collector of these prayers was, first, to have forms of prayer for every day in the week, each of which contained something of deprecation, petition, thanksgiving, and intercession. Second, to have such forms for those days which the Christian church has ever judged peculiarly proper for religious rejoicing, as contained little of deprecation, but were explicit and large in acts of love and thanksgiving. Third, to have such for those days which from the age of the apostles have been set apart for religious mourning, as contained little of thanksgiving, but were full and express in acts of contrition and humiliation. Fourth, to have intercessions every day for all those whom our own church directs us to remember in our prayers. And, fifth, to comprise in the course of petitions for the week the whole scheme of our Christian duty.

Whoever follows the direction of our excellent church in the interpretation of the holy Scriptures, by keeping close to that sense of them which the Catholic fathers and ancient bishops have delivered to succeeding generations, will easily see that the whole system of Christian duty is reducible to these five heads:

First: the renouncing ourselves. "If any man will come after me, let him renounce himself, and follow me" (Matt. 16:24). This implies (1) a thorough conviction that we are not our own; that we are not the proprietors of ourselves or anything we enjoy; that we have no right to dispose of our goods, bodies, souls, or any of the actions or passions of them; (2) a solemn resolution to act suitably to this conviction: not to live to ourselves; not to pursue our own desires; not to please ourselves; nor to suffer our own will to be any principle of action to us.

Second: such a renunciation of ourselves naturally leads to the devoting of ourselves to God. As this implies (1) a thorough conviction that we are God's; that he is the proprietor of all we are and all we have; and that not only by right of creation, but of purchase; for he died for all, and therefore "died for all, that they which live should not henceforth live unto themselves, but unto him that died for them" [2 Cor. 5:15]; (2) a solemn resolution to act suitably to this conviction: to live unto God; to render unto God the things which are God's, even all we are and all we have; to glorify him in our bodies and in our spirits, with all the powers and all the strength of each; and to make his will our sole principle of action.

Third: self-denial is the immediate consequence of this. For whosoever has determined to live no longer to the desires of men, but to the will of God, will soon find that he cannot be true to his purpose without denying himself and taking up his cross daily. He will daily feel some desire which this one principle of action, the will of God, does not require him to indulge. In this, therefore, he must either deny himself, or so far deny the faith. He will daily meet with some means of drawing nearer to God which are unpleasing to flesh and blood. In this, therefore, he must either take up his cross, or so far renounce his Master.

Fourth: by a constant exercise of self-denial, the true follower of Christ continually advances in mortification. He is more and more dead to the world and the things of the world, till at length he can say, with that perfect disciple of his Lord (Marquis de Renty), "I desire nothing but God," or, with St. Paul, "I am crucified unto the world; I am dead with Christ; I live not, but Christ liveth in me" [Gal. 2:20].

Fifth: Christ liveth in me. This is the fulfilling of the law, the last stage of Christian holiness; this maketh the man of God perfect. He that, being dead to the world, is alive to God, the desire of whose soul is unto his name, who has given him his whole heart, who delights in him and in nothing else but what tends to him, who for his sake burns with love toward all mankind, who neither thinks, speaks, nor acts but to fulfill his will is on the last round of the ladder to heaven. Grace hath had its full work upon his soul. The next step he takes is into glory.

May the God of glory give unto us who have not already attained this, neither are already perfect, to do this one thing: "Forgetting those things which are behind, and reaching forth unto those things which are before, to press toward the mark for the prize of our high calling in Christ Jesus!" [Phil. 3:13–14].

May he so enlighten our eyes that "we may reckon all things but loss for the excellency of the knowledge of Christ Jesus our Lord" [Phil. 3:8]; and our hearts that we may rejoice to suffer the loss of all things, and count them but dung, that we may win Christ!

Sunday Evening

General Questions a Serious Christian May Propose to Himself Before He Begins His Evening Devotions

1. With what degree of attention and fervor did I use my morning prayers, public or private?

2. Have I done anything without a present, or at least a previous, perception of its direct or remote tendency to the glory of God?

3. Did I in the morning consider what particular virtue I was to exercise and what business I had to do in the day?

4. Have I been zealous to undertake, and active in doing, what good I could?

5. Have I interested myself any further in the affairs of others than charity required?

6. Have I, before I visited or was visited, considered how I might thereby give or receive improvement?

7. Have I mentioned any failing or fault of any man when it was not necessary for the good of another?

8. Have I unnecessarily grieved anyone by word or deed?

9. Have I before or in every action considered how it might be a means of improving in the virtue of the day?

Particular Questions Relative to the Love of God

1. Have I set apart some of this day to think upon his perfections and mercies?

2.   Have I labored to make this day a day of heavenly rest, sacred to divine love?

3.   Have I employed those parts of it in works of necessity and mercy which were not employed in prayer, reading, and meditation?

O my Father, my God, I am in your hand; and may I rejoice above all things in being so. Do with me what seems good in your sight; only let me love you with all my mind, soul, and strength.

I magnify you for granting me to be born in your church, and of religious parents; for washing me in your baptism, and instructing me in your doctrine of truth and holiness; for sustaining me by your gracious providence, and guiding me by your blessed Spirit; for admitting me, with the rest of my Christian brethren, to wait on you at your public worship; and for so often feeding my soul with your most precious body and blood, those pledges of love and sure conveyances of strength and comfort. Oh, be gracious unto all of us whom you have this day (or at any time) admitted to your holy table. Strengthen our hearts in your ways against all our temptations, and make us "more than conquerors" [Rom. 8:37] in your love.

O my Father, my God, deliver me, I beseech you, from all violent passions. I know how greatly obstructive these are of both the knowledge and the love of you. Oh, let none of them find a way into my heart, but let me ever possess my soul in meekness. O my God, I desire to fear them more than death; let me not serve these cruel tyrants, but do you reign in my breast; let me be ever your servant and love you with all my heart.

Deliver me, O God, from too intense an application to even necessary business. I know how this dissipates my thoughts from the one end of all my business, and impairs that lively perception I would ever retain of your standing at my right hand. I know the narrowness of my heart, and that an eager attention to earthly things leaves it no room for the things of heaven. Oh, teach me to go through all my employments with so truly disengaged a heart that I may still see you in all things, and see you therein as continually looking upon me and searching my reins; and that I may never impair that liberty of spirit which is necessary for the love of you.

Deliver me, O God, from a slothful mind, from all lukewarmness, and all dejection of spirit. I know these cannot but deaden my love to you; mercifully free my heart from them, and give me a lively, zealous, active, and cheerful spirit, that I may vigorously perform whatever you command, thankfully suffer whatever you choose for me, and be ever ardent to obey in all things your holy love.

Deliver me, O God, from all idolatrous love of any creature. I know infinite numbers have been lost to you by loving those creatures for their own sake, which you permit, nay, even command, to love subordinately to you. Preserve me, I beseech you, from all such blind affection; be a guard to all my desires, that they fix on no creature any farther than the love of it tends to build me up in the love of you. You require me to love you with all my heart:

undertake for me, I beseech you, and be my security, that I may never open my heart to anything but out of love to you.

Above all, deliver me, O my God, from all idolatrous self-love. I know, O God (blessed be your infinite mercy for giving me this knowledge) that this is the root of all evil. I know you made me not to do my own will but yours. I know the very corruption of the devil is the having of a will contrary to yours. Oh, be my helper against this most dangerous of all idols, that I may both discern all its subtleties and withstand all its force. O you who have commanded me to renounce myself, give me strength, and I will obey your command. My choice and desire is to love myself, as all other creatures, in and for you. Oh, let your almighty arm so establish, strengthen, and settle me that you may ever be the ground and pillar of all my love.

By this love of you, my God, may my soul be fixed against its natural inconstancy; by this may it be reduced to an entire indifference as to all things else, and simply desire what is pleasing in your sight. May this holy flame ever warm my breast, that I may serve you with all my might; and let it consume in my heart all selfish desires, that I may in all things regard not myself but you.

O my God, let your glorious name be duly honored and loved by all the creatures you have made. Let your infinite goodness and greatness be ever adored by all angels and men. May your church, the Catholic seminary of divine love, be protected from all the powers of darkness. Oh, vouchsafe to all who call themselves by your name one short glimpse of your goodness. May they once taste and see how gracious you are, that all things else may be tasteless to them; that their desires may be always flying up toward you, that they may render to you love, and praise, and obedience, pure and cheerful, constant and zealous, universal and uniform, like that the holy angels render to you in heaven.

Send forth your blessed Spirit into the midst of these sinful nations and make us a holy people. Stir up the heart of our sovereign, of the royal family, of the clergy, the nobility, and of all whom you have set over us, that they may be happy instruments in your hand of promoting this good work. Be gracious to the universities, to the gentry and commons of this land. And comfort all that are in affliction; let the trial of their faith work patience in them, and perfect them in hope and love.

Bless my father, my friends and relations, and all that belong to this family; all that have been instrumental to my good, by their assistance, advice, example, or writing; and all that do not pray for themselves.

Change the hearts of my enemies, and give me grace to forgive them, even as you for Christ's sake forgive us.

O Shepherd of Israel, vouchsafe to receive me this night and ever into your protection; accept my poor services, and pardon the sinfulness of these and all my holy duties. Oh, let it be your good pleasure shortly to put a period to sin and misery, to infirmity and death, to complete the number of your elect, and to hasten your kingdom; that we, and all that wait for your salvation, may eternally love and praise you, O God the Father, God the Son, and God the Holy Ghost, throughout all ages, world without end. Our Father, etc.

Monday Morning

General Questions, Which May Be Used Every Morning.

Did I think of God first and last?

Have I examined myself how I behaved since last night's retirement?

Am I resolved to do all the good I can this day, and to be diligent in the business of my calling?

O God, who are the giver of all good gifts, I, your unworthy servant, entirely desire to praise your name for all the expressions of your bounty toward me. Blessed be your love for giving your Son to die for our sins, for the means of grace, and for the hope of glory. Blessed be your love for all the temporal benefits which you have with a liberal hand poured out upon me; for my health and strength, food and raiment, and all other necessaries with which you have provided your sinful servant. I also bless you that, after all my refusals of your grace, you still have patience with me, have preserved me this night, and given me yet another day to renew and perfect my repentance. Pardon, good Lord, all my former sins, and make me every day more zealous and diligent to improve every opportunity of building up my soul in your faith, and love, and obedience. Make yourself always present to my mind, and let your love fill and rule my soul, in all those places, and companies, and employments to which you call me this day. In all my passage through this world, suffer not my heart to be set upon it; but always fix my single eye and my undivided affections on the "prize of my high calling." This one thing let me do; let me so press toward this as to make all things else minister unto it; and be careful so to use them as thereby to fit my soul for that pure bliss which you have prepared for those that love you.

O you who are good and do good, who extend your loving-kindness to all mankind, the work of your hands, your image, capable of knowing and loving you eternally: suffer me to exclude none, O Lord, from my charity who are the objects of your mercy; but let me treat all my neighbors with that tender love which is due to your servants and to your children. You have required this mark of my love to you. Oh, let no temptation expose me to ingratitude, or make me forfeit your loving-kindness, which is better than life itself. But grant that I may assist all my brethren with my prayers where I cannot reach them with actual services. Make me zealous to embrace all occasions that may administer to their happiness, by assisting the needy, protecting the oppressed, instructing the ignorant, confirming the wavering, exhorting the good, and reproving the wicked. Let me look upon the failings of my neighbor as if they were my own; that I may be grieved for them, that I may never reveal them but when charity requires, and then with tenderness and compassion. Let your love to me, O blessed Savior, be the pattern of my love to him. You thought nothing too dear to part with, to rescue me from eternal misery. Oh, let me think nothing too dear to part with to set forward the everlasting good of my fellow Christians. They are members of your body; therefore I will cherish them. You have redeemed them with an inestimable price; assisted by your Holy Spirit, therefore, I will endeavor to recover them from a state of destruction; that thus adorning your holy gospel, by doing good according to my power, I may at last be received into the endearments of your eternal love, and sing everlasting praise unto the Lamb that was slain and sits on the throne forever.

Extend, I humbly beseech thee, your mercy to all men, and let them become your faithful servants. Let all Christians live up to the holy religion they profess, especially these sinful nations. Be entreated for us, good Lord; be glorified by our reformation, and not by our destruction. "Turn us, and so shall we be turned" [Ps. 80:3]. Oh, be favorable to your people; give us grace to put a period to our provocations, and do put a period to our punishment. Defend our church from schism, heresy, and sacrilege, and the king from all treasons and conspiracies. Bless all bishops, priests, and deacons with apostolic graces, exemplary lives, and sound doctrine. Grant to the council wisdom from above, to all magistrates integrity and zeal, to the universities quietness and industry, and to the gentry and commons pious and peaceable and loyal hearts.

Preserve my parents, my brothers and sisters, my friends and relations, and all mankind in their souls and bodies. Forgive my enemies, and in your due time make them kindly affected toward me. Have mercy on all who are "afflicted in mind, body, or estate; give them patience under their sufferings, and a happy issue out of all their afflictions." Oh, grant that we, with those who are already dead in your faith and fear, may together partake of a joyful resurrection, through him who lives and reigns with you and the Holy Ghost, one God, world without end.

A Scheme of Self-Examination

Used by the First Methodists in Oxford

Sunday

Love of God and Simplicity: Means of Which Are Prayer and Meditation

1. Have I been simple and recollected in everything I said or did? Have I been (a) simple in everything, that is, looked upon God, my Good, my Pattern, my one Desire, my Disposer, Parent of Good; acted wholly for him; bounded my views with the present action or hour? (b) Recollected, that is, has this simple view been distinct and uninterrupted? Have I, in order to keep it so, used the signs agreed upon with my friends, wherever I was? Have I done anything without a previous perception of its being the will of God? Or without a perception of its being an exercise or a means of the virtue of the day? Have I said anything without it?

2. Have I prayed with fervor? At going in and out of church? In the church? Morning and evening in private? Monday, Wednesday, and Friday, with my friends, at rising? Before lying down? On Saturday noon? All the time I am engaged in exterior work in private? Before I go into the place of public or private prayer for help therein? Have I, wherever I was, gone to church morning and evening, unless for necessary mercy, and spent from one hour to three in private? Have I, in private prayer, frequently stopped short and observed what fervor? Have I repeated it over and over, till I adverted to every word? Have I at the beginning of every prayer or paragraph owned I cannot pray? Have I paused before I concluded in his name, and adverted to my

Savior now interceding for me at the right hand of God and offering up these prayers?

3.   Have I duly used ejaculations? That is, have I every hour prayed for humility, faith, hope, love, and the particular virtue of the day? Considered with whom I was the last hour, what I did, and how? With regard to recollection, love of man, humility, self-denial, resignation, and thankfulness? Considered the next hour in the same respects, offered up all I do to my Redeemer, begged his assistance in every particular, and commended my soul to his keeping? Have I done this deliberately, not in haste, seriously, not doing anything else the while, and as fervently as I could?

4.   Have I duly prayed for the virtue of the day? That is, have I prayed for it at going out and coming in? Deliberately, seriously, fervently?

5.   Have I used a collect at nine, twelve, and three? And grace before and after eating? Aloud at my own room? Deliberately, seriously, fervently?

6.   Have I duly meditated? Every day, unless for necessary mercy, (a) from six, etc., to prayers? (b) From four to five? What was particular in the providence of this day? How ought the virtue of the day to have been exerted upon it? How did it fall short? (Here faults.) (c) On Sunday, from six to seven, with Kempis? From three to four on redemption or God's attributes? Wednesday and Friday, from twelve to one, on the Passion? After ending a book, on what I had marked in it?

Monday

Love of Man

1. Have I been zealous to do, and active in doing, good? That is, have I embraced every probable opportunity of doing good, and preventing, removing, or lessening evil? Have I pursued it with my might? Have I thought anything too dear to part with to serve my neighbor? Have I spent an hour at least every day in speaking to someone or other? Have I given anyone up till he expressly renounced me? Have I, before I spoke to any, learned, as far as I could, his temper, way of thinking, past life, and peculiar hindrances, internal and external? Fixed the point to be aimed at? Then the means to it? Have I in speaking proposed the motives, then the difficulties, then balanced them, then exhorted him to consider both calmly and deeply, and to pray earnestly for help? Have I in speaking to a stranger explained what religion is not (not negative, not external) and what it is (a recovery of the image of God)? Searched at what step in it he stops, and what makes him stop there? Exhorted and directed him? Have I persuaded all I could to attend public prayers, sermons, and sacraments, and in general to obey the laws of the church Catholic, the Church of England, the state, the university, and their respective colleges? Have I, when taxed with any act of obedience, avowed it and turned the attack with sweetness and firmness? Have I disputed upon any practical point, unless it was to be practiced just then? Have I in disputing (a) desired him to define the terms of the question; to limit it; what he grants, what denies? (b)

Delayed speaking my opinion; let him explain and prove his; then insinuated and pressed objections? Have I after every visit asked him who went with me, "Did I say anything wrong?" Have I, when anyone asked advice, directed and exhorted him with all my power?

2. Have I rejoiced with and for my neighbor in virtue or pleasure? Grieved with him in pain, for him in sin?

3. Have I received his infirmities with pity, not anger?

4. Have I thought or spoke unkindly of or to him? Have I revealed any evil of anyone, unless it was necessary to some particular good I had in view? Have I then done it with all the tenderness of phrase and manner consistent with that end? Have I anyway appeared to approve them that did otherwise?

5. Has goodwill been, and appeared to be, the spring of all my actions toward others?

6. Have I duly used intercession? Before, after, speaking to any? For my friends on Sunday? For my pupils on Monday? For those who have particularly desired it, on Wednesday and Friday? For the family in which I am, every day?

Advice on Spiritual Reading

Part of the Preface to John Wesley's Abridgment
of Thomas à Kempis's *The Imitation of Christ* (1735)

It is to these alone who, knowing they have not yet attained, neither are already perfect, mind this one thing and, pressing toward the mark, despise no assistance which is offered them, that the following advices are proposed concerning the manner of reading this (or any other religious) treatise.

First: assign some stated time every day for this employment; and observe it, so far as you possibly can, inviolably. But if necessary business, which you could not foresee or defer, should sometimes rob you of your hour of retirement, take the next to it; or, if you cannot have that, at least the nearest you can.

Second: prepare yourself for reading by purity of intention, singly aiming at the good of your soul, and by fervent prayer to God, that he would enable you to see his will and give you a firm resolution to perform it. An excellent form of prayer for this very purpose you have in the second or third book of this treatise.

Third: be sure to read, not cursorily or hastily, but leisurely, seriously, and with great attention, with proper pauses and intervals, and that you may allow time for the enlightenings of the divine grace. To this end, recollect, every now and then, what you have read, and consider how to reduce it to practice. Further, let your reading be continued and regular, not rambling and desultory. To taste of many things without fixing upon any shows a vitiated palate and feeds the disease which makes it pleasing. Whatsoever book you begin, read, therefore, through in order: not but that it will be of great service to read those passages over and over that more nearly concern yourself and more closely affect your inclinations or practice, especially if you press them home to your soul by adding a particular examination of yourself upon each head.

Fourth: labor to work yourself up into a temper correspondent with what you read, for that reading is useless which only enlightens the understanding without warming the affections. And therefore intersperse, here and there, earnest aspirations to God for his heat as well as his light. Select also any remarkable sayings or advices and treasure them up in your memory; and these you may either draw forth in time of need, as arrows from a quiver, against temptation (more especially against the solicitations to that sin which most easily besets you) or make use of as incitements to any virtue, to humility, patience, or the love of God.

Conclude all with a short ejaculation to God, that he, without whom "neither is he that planteth anything, nor he that watereth" [1 Cor. 3:7], would so bless the good seed sown in your heart, that it may bring forth fruit unto life eternal.

Extracts from John Wesley's Journal

January 8 to May 24, 1738

Sunday, January 8

In the fullness of my heart, I wrote the following words.

By the most infallible of proofs, inward feeling, I am convinced:

1. Of unbelief—having no such faith will prevent my heart from being troubled, which it could not be if I believed in God and rightly believed also in [Christ];

2. Of pride throughout my life past, inasmuch as I thought I had what I find I have not;

3. Of gross irrecollection, inasmuch as in a storm I cry to God every moment; in a calm, not;

4. Of levity and luxuriance of spirit, recurring whenever the pressure is taken off; and appearing by my speaking words not tending to edify; but most by my manner of speaking of my enemies.

Lord, save, or I perish! Save me:

1. By such a faith as implies peace in life and in death;

2. By such humility as may fill my heart from this hour forever, with a piercing, uninterrupted sense; *nihil est quod hactenus feci* (I have done nothing hitherto), having evidently built without a foundation;

3. By such a recollection as may cry to thee every moment, especially when all is calm. Give me faith, or I die; give me a lowly spirit: otherwise, *mihi non sit suave vivere* (Let life be a burden to me).

4.   By steadiness, seriousness, sobriety of spirit; avoiding, as fire, every word that tends not to edifying, and never speaking of any who oppose me; or sin against God, without all my own sins set in array before my face.

Tuesday, [January] 24

We spoke with two ships, outward-bound, from whom we had the welcome news of our wanting but one hundred and sixty leagues of the Land's End. My mind was now full of thought, part of which I wrote down as follows.

I went to America to convert the Indians but, oh, who shall convert me? Who, what, is he that will deliver me from this evil heart of unbelief? I have a fair summer religion. I can talk well, nay, and believe myself, while no danger is near. But let death look me in the face, and my spirit is troubled. Nor can I say, "To die is gain" [Phil. 1:21].

I have a sin of fear, that when I've spun
My last thread, I shall perish on the shore!

I think, verily, if the gospel be true, I am safe, for I not only have given and do give all my goods to feed the poor; I not only give my body to be burned, drowned, or whatever God shall appoint for me; but I follow after charity (though not as I ought, yet as I can) if haply I may attain it. I now believe the gospel is true. I "show my faith by my works" [James 2:18] by staking my all upon it. I would do so again and again a thousand times, if the choice were still to make. Whoever sees me, sees I would be a Christian. Therefore "are my ways not like other men's ways"? Therefore, I have been, I am, I am content to be, a "byword, a proverb of reproach." But in a storm I think, "What if the gospel be not true? Then thou art of all men most foolish. For what have you given up your goods, your ease, your friends, your reputation, your country, your life? For what are you wandering over the face of the earth—a dream, a cunningly devised fable? Oh, who will deliver me from this fear of death? What shall I do? Where shall I fly from it? Should I fight against it by thinking or by not thinking of it?" A wise man advised me some time since, "Be still and go on." Perhaps this is best, to look upon it as my cross; when it comes, to let it humble me and quicken all my good resolutions, especially that of praying without ceasing, and at other times to take no thought about it, but quietly go on in the work of the Lord.

For many years I have been tossed by various winds of doctrine. I asked long ago, "What must I do to be saved"? The Scripture answered, "Keep the commandments, believe, hope, love; follow after these tempers till you have fully attained (that is, till death) by all those outward works and means which God has appointed, by walking as Christ walked."

I was early warned against laying, as the papists do, too much stress on outward works—or on a faith without works, which, as it does not include, so it will never lead to, true hope or charity. Nor am I sensible that to this hour I have laid too much stress on either, having from the very beginning valued both faith and the means of grace and good works not on their own account, but as believing that God, who had appointed them, would by them bring me in due time to the mind that was in Christ.

But before God's time was come, I fell among some Lutheran and Calvinist authors whose confused and undigested accounts magnified faith to such an amazing size that it quite hid all the rest of the commandments. I did not then see that this was the natural effect of their overgrown fear of popery, being so terrified with the cry of merit and good works that they plunged at once into the other extreme. In this labyrinth I was utterly lost, not being able to find out what the error was, nor yet to reconcile this uncouth hypothesis either with Scripture or common sense.

The English writers, such as Bishop Beveridge, Bishop Taylor, and Mr. Nelson, a little relieved me from these well-meaning, wrongheaded Germans. Their accounts of Christianity I could easily see to be, in the main, consistent both with reason and Scripture. Only when they interpreted Scripture in different ways I was often much at a loss. And again, there was one thing much insisted on in Scripture—the unity of the church—which none of them, I thought, clearly explained or strongly inculcated.

But it was not long before Providence brought me to those who showed me a sure rule of interpreting Scripture, viz.: *Consensus veterum: quod ab omnibus, quod ubique, quod semper creditum* (The consensus of antiquity: that which has been believed by everyone, everywhere, and always). At the same time they sufficiently insisted upon a due regard to the one church at all times and in all places.

Nor was it long before I bent the bow too far the other way:

1. By making antiquity a coordinate rather than subordinate rule with Scripture.

2. By admitting several doubtful writings as undoubted evidences of antiquity.

3. By extending antiquity too far, even to the middle or end of the fourth century.

4. By believing more practices to have been universal in the ancient church than ever were so.

5. By not considering that the decrees of one provincial synod could bind only that province; and that the decrees of a general synod [bound] only those provinces whose representatives met therein.

6. By not considering that most of those decrees were adapted to particular times and occasions and, consequently, when these occasions ceased, must cease to bind even those provinces.

These considerations insensibly stole upon me as I grew acquainted with the mystic writers, whose noble descriptions of union with God and internal religion made everything else appear mean, flat, and insipid. But, in truth, they made good works appear so, too; yea, and faith itself, and what not?

Wednesday, May 24

What occurred on Wednesday 24th (May), I think best to relate at large, after premising what may make it the better understood. Let him that cannot receive it. ask the Father of lights that he would give more light both to him and me.

I believe, till I was about ten years old, I had not sinned away that washing of the Holy Ghost which was given me in baptism, having been strictly educated and carefully taught that I could only be saved by universal obedience, by keeping all the commandments of God—in the meaning of which I was diligently instructed. And those instructions, so far as they respected outward duties and sins, I gladly received and often thought of. But all that was said to me of inward obedience or holiness I neither understood nor remembered. So that I was indeed as ignorant of the true meaning of the law as I was of the gospel of Christ.

The next six or seven years were spent at school, where, outward restraints being removed, I was much more negligent than before, even of outward duties, and almost continually guilty of outward sins which I knew to be such, though they were not scandalous in the eye of the world. However, I still read the Scriptures and said my prayers, morning and evening. And what I now hoped to be saved by was (1) not being so bad as other people; (2) having still a kindness for religion; and (3) reading the Bible, going to church, and saying my prayers.

Being removed to the university for five years, I still said my prayers both in public and in private and read with the Scriptures several other books of religion, especially comments on the New Testament. Yet I had not all this while so much as a notion of inward holiness, nay, went on habitually, and for the most part very contentedly, in some or other known sin—indeed, with some intermissions and short struggles, especially before and after the Holy Communion, which I was obliged to receive thrice a year. I cannot well tell what I hoped to be saved by now, when I was continually sinning against that little light I had, unless by those transient fits of what many divines taught me to call "repentance."

When I was about twenty-two, my father pressed me to enter into Holy Orders. At the same time, the providence of God directing me to Kempis's *Christian Pattern*, I began to see that true religion was seated in the heart and that God's law extended to all our thoughts as well as words and actions. I was, however, very angry at Kempis for being *too* strict, though I read him only in Dean Stanhope's translation. Yet I had frequently much sensible comfort in reading him such as I was an utter stranger to before. Meeting likewise with a religious friend, which I never had till now, I began to alter the whole form of my conversation and to set in earnest upon "a new life." I set apart an hour or two a day for religious retirement. I communicated every week. I watched against all sin, whether in word or deed. I began to aim at, and pray for, inward holiness. So that now, doing so much and living so good a life, I doubted not but I was a good Christian.

Removing soon after to another college, I executed a resolution which I was before convinced was of the utmost importance—

shaking off at once all my trifling acquaintance. I began to see more and more the value of time. I applied myself closer to study. I watched more carefully against actual sins. I advised others to be religious, according to that scheme of religion by which I modeled my own life. But meeting now with Mr. Law's *Christian Perfection* and *Serious Call* (although I was much offended at many parts of both, yet), they convinced me more than ever of the exceeding height and breadth and depth of the law of God. The light flowed in so mightily upon my soul that everything appeared in a new view. I cried to God for help and resolved not to prolong the time of obeying him, as I had never done before. And by my continued endeavor to keep his whole law, inward and outward, to the utmost of my power, I was persuaded that I should be accepted of him and that I was even then in a state of salvation.

In 1730 I began visiting the prisons, assisting the poor and sick in town, and doing what other good I could by my presence or my little fortune to the bodies and souls of all men. To this end I abridged myself of all superfluities, and many that are called necessaries of life. I soon became a "byword" for so doing, and I rejoiced that "my name was cast out as evil" [Luke 6:22]. The next spring I began observing the Wednesday and Friday fasts commonly observed in the ancient church, tasting no food till three in the afternoon. And now I knew not how to go any further. I diligently strove against all sin. I omitted no sort of self-denial which I thought lawful. I carefully used, both in public and private, all the means of grace at all opportunities. I omitted no occasion of doing good. I for that reason suffered evil. And all this I knew to be nothing unless as it was directed toward inward holiness. Accordingly this, the image of God, was what I aimed at in all, by doing his will, not my own. Yet when, after continuing some years in this course, I apprehended myself to be near death, I could not find that all this gave me any comfort or any assurance of acceptance with God. At this I was then not a little surprised, not imagining I had been all this time building on the sand, nor considering that "other foundation can no man lay than that which is laid by God, even Christ Jesus" [1 Cor. 3:11].

Soon after, a contemplative man convinced me still more than I was convinced before that outward works are nothing, being alone, and in several conversations instructed me how to pursue inward holiness, or a union of the soul with God. But even of his instructions (though I then received them as the words of God) I cannot but now observe (a) that he spoke so incautiously against trusting in outward works that he discouraged me from doing them at all; (b) that he recommended (as it were, to supply what was wanting in them) mental prayer and the like exercises as the most effectual means of purifying the soul and uniting it with God. Now these were, in truth, as much my own works as visiting the sick or clothing the naked; and the "union with God" thus pursued was as really my own righteousness as any I had before pursued under another name.

In this refined way of trusting to my own works and my own righteousness (so zealously inculcated by the mystic writers), I dragged on heavily, finding no comfort or help therein till the time of my leaving England. On shipboard, however, I was again active in outward works, where it pleased God of his free mercy to give me twenty-six of the Moravian brethren for companions, who endeavored to show me a more excellent way. But I understood it not at first. I was too learned and too wise, so that it seemed foolishness unto me. And I continued preaching and following after and trusting in that righteousness whereby no flesh can be justified.

All the time I was at Savannah I was thus beating the air. Being ignorant of the righteousness of Christ, which, by a living faith in him, bringeth salvation to "every one that believeth" [Rom. 1:16]. I sought to establish my own righteousness, and so labored in the fire all my days. I was now properly "under the law." I knew that "the law" of God was "spiritual; I consented to it that it was good." Yea, "I delighted in it after the inner man." Yet was I "carnal, sold under sin." Every day was I constrained to cry out, "What I do, I allow not: for what I would, I do not; but what I hate, that I do. To will is indeed present with me; but how to perform that which is good, I find not. For the good which I would, I do not, but the evil which I would not, that I do. I find a law that when I would do good, evil is present with me, even the law in my members, warring against the law of my mind and still bringing me into captivity to the law of sin" [Rom. 7:14–23].

In this state I was indeed fighting continually, but not conquering. Before, I had willingly served sin; now it was unwillingly, but still I served it. I fell and rose and fell again. Sometimes I was overcome and in heaviness; sometimes I overcame and was in joy. For as in the former state I had some foretastes of the terrors of the law, so had I in this of the comforts of the gospel. During this

whole struggle between nature and grace which had now continued above ten years, I had many remarkable returns to prayer,
especially when I was in trouble. I had many sensible comforts,
which are indeed no other than short anticipations of the life of
faith. But I was still "under the law," not "under grace" (the state
most who are called Christians are content to live and die in), for
I was only "striving with, not freed from, sin." Neither had I "the
witness of the Spirit with my spirit," and indeed could not, for I
"sought it not by faith, but as it were by the works of the law"
[Rom. 6:7, 14; 8:16, 9:32].

In my return to England, January 1738, being in imminent
danger of death and very uneasy on that account, I was strongly
convinced that the cause of that uneasiness was unbelief and that
the gaining a true, living faith was the one thing needful for me.
But still I fixed not this faith in its right object: I meant only faith
in God, not faith in or through Christ. Again, I knew not that I
was *wholly void of this faith*, but only thought *I had not enough* of it. So
that when Peter Böhler, whom God prepared for me as soon as I
came to London, affirmed of true faith in Christ (which is but
one) that it had those two fruits inseparably attending it, "dominion over sin, and constant peace from a sense of forgiveness," I
was quite amazed and looked upon it as a new gospel. If this was
so, it was clear I had not faith. But I was not willing to be convinced of this. Therefore I disputed with all my might and labored
to prove that faith might be where these were not, especially
where the sense of forgiveness was not; for all the scriptures
relating to this I had been long since taught to construe away and

to call all Presbyterians who spoke otherwise. Besides, I well saw no one could, in the nature of things, have such a sense of forgiveness and not feel it. But I felt it not. If, then, there was no faith without this, all my pretensions to faith dropped at once.

When I met Peter Böhler again, he consented to put the dispute upon the issue which I desired, namely, Scripture and experience. I first consulted the Scripture. But when I set aside the glosses of men and simply considered the words of God, comparing them together, endeavoring to illustrate the obscure by the plainer passages, I found they all made against me and was forced to retreat to my last hold, "that experience would never agree with the *literal interpretation* of those scriptures. Nor could I therefore allow it to be true, till I found some living witnesses of it." He replied he could show me such at any time; if I desired it, the next day. And, accordingly, the next day he came again with three others, all of whom testified of their own personal experience that a true living faith in Christ is inseparable from a sense of pardon for all past and freedom from all present sins. They added with one mouth that this faith was the gift, the free gift of God, and that he would surely bestow it upon every soul who earnestly and perseveringly sought it. I was not thoroughly convinced and, by the grace of God, I resolved to seek it unto the end, first, by absolutely renouncing all dependence, in whole or in part, upon my own works or righteousness—on which I had really grounded my hope of salvation, though I knew it not, from my youth up; second, by adding to "the constant use of all the 'other' means of grace," continual prayer for this very thing—justifying, saving faith, a full reliance on the blood of Christ shed for me, a trust in him, as my Christ, as my sole justification, sanctification, and redemption.

I continued thus to seek it (though with strange indifference, dullness and coldness and unusually frequent relapses into sin) till Wednesday, May 24. I think it was about five this morning, that I opened my Testament on those words, "There are given unto us exceeding great and precious promises, even that you should be partakers of the divine nature" (2 Pet. 1:4). Just as I went out, I opened it again on those words, "You are not far from the kingdom of God" [Mark 12:34]. In the afternoon I was asked to go to St. Paul's. The anthem was "Out of the deep have I called unto you, O Lord: Lord, hear my voice. O let your ears consider well the voice of my complaint. If you, Lord, will be extreme to mark what is done amiss, O Lord, who may abide it? For there is mercy with you; therefore shall you be feared. O Israel, trust in the Lord, for with the Lord there is mercy and with him is plenteous redemption. And he shall redeem Israel from all his sins" [Ps. 130].

In the evening, I went very unwillingly to a society in Aldersgate Street, where one was reading Luther's Preface to the Epistle to the Romans. About a quarter before nine, while he was describing the change which God works in the heart through faith in Christ, I felt my heart strangely warmed. I felt I did trust in Christ, Christ alone for salvation; and an assurance was given me that he had taken away my sins, even mine, and saved me from the law of sin and death.

I began to pray with all my might for those who had in a more especial manner despitefully used me and persecuted me. I then testified openly to all there what I now first felt in my heart. But it was not long before the enemy suggested, "This cannot be faith, for where is your joy?" Then was I taught that "peace and victory over sin are essential to faith in the Captain of our salvation but that, as to the transports of joy—that usually attend the beginning of it especially in those who have mourned deeply—God sometimes giveth, sometimes withholdest them, according to the counsels of his own will."

After my return home, I was much buffeted with temptations, but cried out and they fled away. They returned again and again. I as often lifted up my eyes and he "sent me help from his holy place" [Ps. 20:2]. And herein I found [in what] the difference between this and my former state chiefly consisted. I was striving, yea, fighting with all my might under the law, as well as under grace. But then I was sometimes, if not often, conquered; now, I was always conqueror.

A Meditation on the Lord's Prayer

An Extract from Wesley's Sermon on the Mount VI
(first published 1748)

After having taught the true nature and ends of prayer, our Lord subjoins an example of it; even that divine form of prayer which seems in this place to be proposed by way of pattern chiefly, as the model and standard of all our prayers: "After this manner therefore pray ye" [Matt. 6:9]. Whereas elsewhere he enjoins the use of these very words: "He said unto them, When you pray, say—" (Luke 11:2).

We may observe, in general, concerning this divine prayer, first, that it contains all we can reasonably or innocently pray for. There is nothing which we have need to ask of God, nothing which we can ask without offending him, which is not included, either directly or indirectly, in this comprehensive form. Second, that it contains all we can reasonably or innocently desire; whatever is for the glory of God, whatever is needful or profitable, not only for ourselves, but for every creature in heaven and earth. And, indeed, our prayers are the proper test of our desires, nothing being fit to have a place in our desires which is not fit to have a place in our prayers: what we may not pray for, neither should we desire. Third, that it contains all our duty to God and man; whatsoever things are pure and holy, whatsoever God requires of the children of men, whatsoever is acceptable in his sight, whatsoever it is whereby we may profit our neighbor being expressed or implied therein.

It consists of three parts—the preface, the petitions, and the doxology, or conclusion. The preface, "Our Father who are in heaven," lays a general foundation for prayer, comprising what we must first know of God before we can pray in confidence of being heard. It likewise points out to us all those tempers with

which we are to approach to God, which are most essentially req-
uisite, if we desire either our prayers or our lives should find
acceptance with him.

Our Father. If he is a father, then he is good, then he is loving, to
his children. And here is the first and great reason for prayer. God
is willing to bless; let us ask for a blessing. "Our Father": our
Creator, the Author of our being; he who raised us from the dust
of the earth, who breathed into us the breath of life, and we
became living souls. But if he made us, let us ask, and he will not
withhold any good thing from the work of his own hands. "Our
Father": our Preserver; who, day by day, sustains the life he has
given, of whose continuing love we now and every moment
receive life and breath and all things. So much the more boldly
let us come to him, and we shall "obtain mercy, and find grace
to help in time of need" [Heb. 4:16]. Above all, the Father of our
Lord Jesus Christ, and of all that believe in him; who justifies us
"freely by his grace, through the redemption that is in Jesus";
who has "blotted out all our sins, and healed all our infirmities";
who has received us for his own children, by adoption and
grace, and, "because we are sons, has sent forth the Spirit of his
Son into our hearts, crying, Abba, Father"; who "has begotten us
again of incorruptible seed" and "created us anew in Christ
Jesus" [Rom. 3:24; 4:7; Gal. 4:6; 1 Pet. 1:23; 2 Cor. 5:17].
Therefore we know that he hears us always; therefore we pray to
him without ceasing. We pray, because we love; and "we love
him because he first loved us" [1 John 4:19].

Our Father. Not mine only who now cry unto him, but ours in the most extensive sense. The God and "Father of the spirits of all flesh" [Num. 27:16]; the Father of angels and men: so the very heathens acknowledge him to be the Father of the universe, of all the families both in heaven and earth. Therefore with him there is no respect of persons. He loves all that he has made. "He is loving unto every man, and his mercy is over all his works" [Ps. 145:9]. And the Lord's delight is in them that fear him and put their trust in his mercy, in them that trust in him through the Son of his love, knowing they are "accepted in the Beloved" [Eph. 1:6]. But if God so loved us, we ought also to love one another, yea, all mankind, seeing "God so loved the world that he gave his only begotten Son," even to die the death, that they "might not perish, but have everlasting life" [John 3:16].

Who are in heaven. High and lifted up, God over all, blessed forever: who, sitting on the circle of the heavens, beholds all things both in heaven and earth; whose eye pervades the whole sphere of created being, yea, and of uncreated night; unto whom "are known all his works" and all the works of every creature, not only "from the beginning of the world" (a poor, low, weak translation) but from all "eternity" [Acts 15:18], from everlasting to everlasting; who constrains the host of heaven, as well as the children of men, to cry out with wonder and amazement, Oh, the depth! "The depth of the riches, both of the wisdom and of the knowledge of God!" [Rom. 11:33]. "Who are in heaven": The Lord and Ruler of all, superintending and disposing all things; who are the King of kings, and Lord of lords, the blessed and only Potentate; who are strong and girded about with power, doing whatsoever pleases you; the Almighty; for whensoever you will, to do is present with you. "In heaven": eminently there. Heaven is your throne, "the place where your honor" particularly "dwells" [Ps. 26:8]. But not there alone, for you fill heaven and earth, the whole expanse of space. "Heaven and earth are full of your glory. Glory be to you, O Lord most high!"

Therefore should we "serve the Lord with fear, and rejoice unto him with reverence" [Heb. 12:28]. Therefore should we think, speak, and act, as continually under the eye, in the immediate presence, of the Lord, the King.

Hallowed be your name. This is the first of the six petitions whereof the prayer itself is composed. The name of God is God himself, the nature of God so far as it can be discovered to man. It means therefore, together with his existence, all his attributes or perfections: his eternity, particularly signified by his great and incommunicable name, JEHOVAH, as the apostle John translates it: "The Alpha and Omega, the beginning and the end; he which is, and which was, and which is to come" [Rev. 1:8]; his fullness of being, denoted by his other great name, "I AM THAT I AM!" [Exod. 3:14]—his omnipresence; —his omnipotence; who is indeed the only Agent in the material world, all matter being essentially dull and inactive and moving only as it is moved by the finger of God; and he is the spring of action in every creature, visible and invisible, which could neither act nor exist

without the continual influx and agency of his almighty power;
—his wisdom, clearly deduced from the things that are seen,
from the goodly order of the universe; —his Trinity in Unity,
and Unity in Trinity, discovered to us in the very first line of his
written word, literally, "the Gods created," a plural noun joined
with a verb of the singular number, as well as in every part of his
subsequent revelations given by the mouth of all of his holy
prophets and apostles; —his essential purity and holiness; —
and, above all, his love, which is the very brightness of his glory.

In praying that God, or his name, may be hallowed or glorified, we pray that he may be known, such as he is, by all that are
capable thereof, by all intelligent beings, and with affections suit-
able to that knowledge; that he may be duly honored, and feared,
and loved, by all in heaven above and in the earth beneath, by all
angels and men, whom for that end he has made capable of
knowing and loving him to eternity.

Your kingdom come. This has a close connection with the preceding petition. In order that the name of God might be hallowed,
we pray that his kingdom, the kingdom of Christ, may come.
This kingdom then comes to a particular person, when he
"repents and believes the gospel" [Mark 1:15], when he is
taught of God not only to know himself, but to know Jesus
Christ and him crucified. As "this is life eternal, to know the only
true God, and Jesus Christ whom he hath sent" [John 17:3], so
it is the kingdom of God begun below, set up in the believer's
heart; "the Lord God Omnipotent" then "reigns" [Rev. 19:6]

when he is known through Christ Jesus. He takes unto himself his mighty power, that he may subdue all things unto himself. He goes on in the soul conquering and to conquer till he has put all things under his feet, till "every thought is brought into captivity to the obedience of Christ" [2 Cor. 10:5].

When therefore God shall "give his Son the Heathen for his inheritance, and the uttermost parts of the earth for his possession"; when "all kingdoms shall bow before him, and all nations shall do him service"; when "the mountain of the Lord's house," the church of Christ, "shall be established in the top of the mountains"; when "the fullness of the Gentiles shall come in, and all Israel shall be saved"; then shall it be seen that "the Lord is King," and has put on "glorious apparel," appearing to every soul of man as King of kings and Lord of lords [Ps. 2:8; 72:11; Isa. 2:2; Rom. 11:25–26; Ps. 10:16; Isa. 63:1]. And it is meet for all those who love his appearing to pray that he would hasten the time; that this his kingdom, the kingdom of grace, may come quickly and swallow up all the kingdoms of the earth; that all mankind, receiving him for their King, truly believing in his name, may be filled with righteousness, and peace, and joy, with holiness and happiness, till they are removed hence into his heavenly kingdom, there to reign with him forever and ever.

For this also we pray in those words, "Your kingdom come": we pray for the coming of his everlasting kingdom, the kingdom of glory in heaven, which is the continuation and perfection of the kingdom of grace on earth. Consequently this, as well as the preceding petition, is offered up for the whole intelligent creation, who are all interested in this grand event, the final renovation of all things, by God's putting an end to misery and sin, to infirmity and death, taking all things into his own hands, and setting up the kingdom which endures throughout all ages.

Exactly answerable to all this are those awful words in the prayer at the burial of the dead: "Beseeching you; that it may please you of your gracious goodness, shortly to accomplish the number of your elect, and to hasten your kingdom; that we, with all those that are departed in the true faith of your holy name, may have our perfect consummation and bliss, both in body and soul, in your everlasting glory."

Your will be done in earth, as it is in heaven. This is the necessary and immediate consequence wherever the kingdom of God is come, wherever God dwells in the soul by faith and Christ reigns in the heart by love.

It is probable, many, perhaps the generality of men, at the first view of these words, are apt to imagine they are only an expression of, or petition for, resignation, for a readiness to suffer the will of God, whatsoever it be, concerning us. And this is unquestionably a divine and excellent temper, a most precious gift of God. But this is not what we pray for in this petition, at least, not in the chief and primary sense of it. We pray not so much for a passive, as for an active, conformity to the will of God, in saying, "Your will be done in earth, as it is in heaven."

How is it done by the angels of God in heaven, those who now circle in his throne rejoicing? They do it willingly; they love his commandments and gladly hearken to his words. It is their meat and drink to do his will; it is their highest glory and joy. They do it *continually*; there is no interruption in their willing service. They rest not day or night, but employ every hour (speaking after the manner of men; otherwise our measures of duration, days, and nights, and hours, have no place in eternity) in fulfilling his commands, in executing his designs, in performing the counsel of his will. And they do it *perfectly*. No sin, no defect belongs to angelic minds. It is true, "the stars are not pure in his sight" [Job 25:5], even the morning stars that sing together before him. "In his sight," that is, in comparison of him, the very angels are not pure. But this does not imply that they are not pure in *themselves*. Doubtless they are; they are without spot and blameless. They are altogether devoted to his will and perfectly obedient in all things.

If we view this in another light, we may observe the angels of God in heaven do *all* the will of God. And they do nothing else, nothing but what they are absolutely assured is his will. Again, they do all the will of God *as* willed; in the manner which pleases him, and no other. Yea, and they do this only *because* it is his will; for this end, and no other reason.

When therefore we pray that the will of God may "be done in earth as it is in heaven," the meaning is that all the inhabitants of the earth, even the whole race of mankind, may do the will of their Father, which is in heaven, as *willingly* as the holy angels; that these may do it *continually*, even as they, without any interruption of their willing service; yea, and that they may do it *perfectly*, that "the God of peace, through the blood of the everlasting covenant, may make them perfect in every good work to do his will, and work in them" all "which is well-pleasing in his sight" [Heb. 13:20–21].

In other words, we pray that we and all mankind may do the whole will of God in all things, and nothing else, not the least thing but what is the holy and acceptable will of God. We pray that we may do the whole will of God as he wills, in the manner that pleases him. And, last, that we may do it because it is his will; that this may be the sole reason and ground, the whole and only motive, of whatsoever we think or whatsoever we speak or do.

Give us this day our daily bread. In the three former petitions we have been praying for all mankind. We come now more particularly to desire a supply for our own wants. Not that we are directed, even here, to confine our prayer altogether to ourselves; but this, and each of the following petitions, may be used for the whole church of Christ upon earth.

By "bread" we may understand all things needful, whether for our souls or bodies—the things pertaining to life and godliness. We understand not barely the outward bread, what our Lord terms "the meat which perisheth," but much more the spiritual bread, the grace of God, the food "which endures unto everlasting life" [John 6:27]. It was the judgment of many of the ancient fathers that we are here to understand the sacramental bread also, daily received in the beginning by the whole church of Christ and highly esteemed, till the love of many waxed cold, as the grand channel whereby the grace of his Spirit was conveyed to the souls of all the children of God.

Our daily bread. The word we render "daily" has been differently explained by different commentators. But the most plain and natural sense of it seems to be this, which is retained in almost all translations, as well ancient as modern: what is sufficient for this day, and so for each day as it succeeds.

Give us. For we claim nothing of right, but only of free mercy. We deserve not the air we breathe, the earth that bears, or the sun that shines upon us. All our desert, we own, is hell. But God loves us freely; therefore, we ask him to give what we can no more procure for ourselves than we can merit it at his hands.

Not that either the goodness or the power of God is a reason for us to stand idle. It is his will that we should use all diligence in all things, that we should employ our utmost endeavors, as much as if our success were the natural effect of our own wisdom and strength. And then, as though we had done nothing, we are to depend on him, the giver of every good and perfect gift.

This day. For we are to take no thought for the morrow. For this very end has our wise Creator divided life into these little portions of time, so clearly separated from each other that we might look on every day as a fresh gift of God, another life which we may devote to his glory; and that every evening may be as the close of life, beyond which we are to see nothing but eternity.

And forgive us our trespasses, as we forgive them that trespass against us. As nothing but sin can hinder the bounty of God from flowing forth upon every creature, so this petition naturally follows the former, that, all hindrances being removed, we may the more clearly trust in the God of love for every manner of thing which is good.

Our trespasses. The word properly signifies "our debts." Thus our sins are frequently represented in Scripture; every sin laying us under a fresh debt to God, to whom we already owe, as it were, ten thousand talents. What, then, can we answer when he shall say, "Pay me what you owe" [Matt. 18:28]? We are utterly insolvent; we have nothing to pay; we have wasted all our substance. Therefore, if he deal with us according to the rigor of his law, if he exact what he justly may, he must command us to be "bound hand and foot" and "delivered over to the tormentors" [Matt. 22:13; 18:34].

Indeed, we are already bound hand and foot by the chains of our own sins. These, considered with regard to ourselves, are chains of iron and fetters of brass. They are wounds wherewith the world, the flesh, and the devil have gashed and mangled us all over. They are diseases that drink up our blood and spirits, that bring us down to the chambers of the grave. But, considered as they are here, with regard to God, they are debts immense and numberless. Well, therefore, seeing we have nothing to pay, may we cry unto him, that he would frankly forgive us all!

The word translated "forgive" implies either to forgive a debt or to unloose a chain. And, if we attain the former, the latter follows of course: if our debts are forgiven, the chains fall off our hands. As soon as ever, through the free grace of God in Christ, we "receive forgiveness of sins," we receive likewise "a lot among those which are sanctified by faith which is in him" [Acts 26:18].

Sin has lost its power: it has no dominion over those who are under grace, that is, in favor with God. As "there is now no condemnation to them that are in Christ Jesus" [Rom. 8:1], so they are freed from sin as well as from guilt. "The righteousness of the law is fulfilled in" them, and they "walk not after the flesh but after the Spirit" [Rom. 8:4].

As we forgive them that trespass against us. In these words our Lord clearly declares both on what condition and in what degree or manner we may look to be forgiven of God. All our trespasses and sins are forgiven us, if we forgive, and *as* we forgive, others. This is a point of the utmost importance. And our blessed Lord is so jealous lest at any time we should let it slip out of our thoughts that he not only inserts it in the body of his prayer, but presently after repeats it twice over. "If," says he, "you forgive men their trespasses, your heavenly Father will also forgive you: But if you forgive not men their trespasses, neither will your Father forgive your trespasses" ([Matt. 6:]14–15). Second, God forgives us as we forgive others. So that if any malice or bitterness, if any taint of unkindness or anger remains, if we do not clearly, fully, and from the heart forgive all men their trespasses, we so far cut short the forgiveness of our own: God cannot clearly and fully forgive us; he may show us some degree of mercy; but we will not suffer him to blot out all our sins and forgive all our iniquities.

In the meantime, while we do not from our hearts forgive our neighbor his trespasses, what manner of prayer are we offering to

God whenever we utter these words? We are indeed setting God at open defiance; we are daring him to do his worst. "Forgive us our trespasses, as we forgive them that trespasses against us." That is, in plain terms, "Do not forgive us at all. We desire no favor at your hands. We pray that you will keep our sins in remembrance, and that your wrath may abide upon us." But can you seriously offer such a prayer to God? And has he not yet cast you quick into hell? Oh, tempt him no longer! Now, even now, by his grace, forgive as you would be forgiven! Now have compassion on your fellow servant, as God has had, and will have, pity on you!

And lead us not into temptation, but deliver us from evil. "And lead us not into temptation." The word translated "temptation" means trial of any kind. And so the English word "temptation" was formerly taken in an indifferent sense, although now it is usually understood of solicitation to sin. St. James uses the word in both these senses; first, in its general, then in its restrained, acceptation. He takes it in the former sense when he says, "Blessed is the man that endures temptation: For when he is tried," or approved of God, "he shall receive the crown of life" (James 1:12). He immediately adds, taking the word in the latter sense, "Let no man say, when he is tempted, I am tempted of God: For God cannot be tempted with evil, neither tempts he any man: But every man is tempted when he is drawn away of his own lust," or desire—drawn out of God, in whom alone he is safe—"and enticed," caught as a fish with bait [James 1:13–14]. Then it is, when he is thus "drawn away and enticed," that he properly enters into temptation. Then temptation covers him as a cloud; it overspreads his whole soul. Then how hardly shall he escape out of the snare! Therefore, we beseech God "not to lead us into temptation," that is (seeing God tempts no man), not to suffer us to be led into it. "But deliver us from evil": rather, "from the evil one," "the wicked one," emphatically so called, the prince and god of this world, who works with mighty power in the children of disobedience. But all those who are the children of God by faith are delivered out of his hands. He may fight against them; and so he will. But he cannot conquer, unless they betray their own souls. He may torment for a time, but he cannot destroy, for God is on their side, who will not fail, in the end, to "avenge his own elect, that cry unto him day and night" [Luke 18:7]. Lord, when we are tempted, suffer us not to enter into temptation! Do you make a way for us to escape that the wicked one touch us not!

For yours is the kingdom, the power, and the glory forever and ever. Amen. The conclusion of this divine prayer, commonly called the doxology, is a solemn thanksgiving, a compendious acknowledgment of the attributes and works of God. "For yours is the kingdom"—the sovereign right of all things that are, or ever were, created; yes, your kingdom is an everlasting kingdom, and your dominion endures throughout all ages. "The power"—the executive power whereby you govern all things in your everlasting kingdom, whereby you do whatsoever

pleases you, in all places of your dominion. "And the glory"—
the praise due from every creature, for your power, and the
mightiness of your kingdom, and for all your wondrous works
which you work from everlasting and shall do, world without
end, "forever and ever! Amen!" So be it!

THE HYMNS OF
CHARLES WESLEY

Preface from the 1780 Handbook

For many years I have been importuned to publish such a hymn book as might be generally used in all our congregations throughout Great Britain and Ireland. I have hitherto withstood the importunity, as I believed such a publication was needless, considering the various hymn books which my brother and I have published within these forty years last past, so that it may be doubted whether any religious community in the world has a greater variety of them.

But it has been answered, such a publication is highly needful upon this very account; for the greater part of the people, being poor, are not able to purchase so many books. And those that have purchased them are, as it were, bewildered in the immense variety. There is therefore still wanting a proper collection of hymns for general use, carefully made out of all these books, and one comprised in so moderate a compass as neither to be cumbersome nor expensive.

Such a hymn book you have now before you. It is not so large as to be either cumbersome or expensive. And it is large enough to contain such a variety of hymns as will not soon be worn threadbare. It is large enough to contain all the important truths of our most holy religion, whether speculative or practical, yea, to illustrate them all and to prove them both by Scripture and reason.

May I be permitted to add a few words with regard to the poetry? Then I will speak to those who are judges thereof with all freedom and unreserve. To these I may say, without offense: (a) In these hymns there is no doggerel, no botches, nothing put in to patch up the rhyme, no feeble expletives. (b) Here is nothing turgid or bombast on the one hand, nor low and creeping on the other. (c) Here are no *cant* expressions, no words without meaning. Those who impute this to us know not what they say. We talk common sense (whether they understand it or not) both in verse and prose, and use no word but in a fixed and determinate sense. (d) Here are (allow me to say) both the purity, the strength, and the elegance of the English language—and at the same time the utmost simplicity and plainness, suited to every capacity. Last, I desire men of taste to judge—these are the only competent judges—whether there is not in some of the following verses the true spirit of poetry such as cannot be acquired by art and labor, but must be the gift of nature. By labor a man may become a tolerable imitator of Spenser, Shakespeare, or Milton and may heap together pretty compound epithets as "pale-eyed," "meek-eyed," and the like. But unless he is born a poet, he will never attain the genuine *spirit of poetry.*

But to return. What is of infinitely more moment than the spirit of poetry is the spirit of piety. And I trust all persons of real judgment will find this breathing through the whole collection. It is in this view chiefly that I would recommend it to every truly pious reader: as a means of raising or quickening the spirit of devotion, of confirming his faith, of enlivening his hope, and of kindling or increasing his love to God and man. When poetry thus keeps its place, as the handmaid of piety, it shall attain not a poor perishable wreath, but a crown that fades not away.

Praise and Worship

Oh, for a Thousand Tongues to Sing

Oh, for a thousand tongues to sing
     My dear Redeemer's praise!
The glories of my God and King,
     The triumphs of his grace!

My gracious Master, and my God,
     Assist me to proclaim,
To spread through all the earth abroad
     The honors of thy name.

Jesus, the name that charms our fears,
     That bids our sorrows cease—
'Tis music in the sinner's ears,
     'Tis life, and health, and peace.

He breaks the power of canceled sin,
     He sets the prisoner free;
His blood can make the foulest clean—
     His blood availed for me.

Hear him, ye deaf; his praise, ye dumb,
     Your loosened tongues employ;
Ye blind, behold your Savior come,
     And leap, ye lame, for joy!

Look unto him, ye nations, own
     Your God, ye fallen race;

Look, and be saved through faith alone,
    Be justified by grace.

See all your sins on Jesus laid:
    The Lamb of God was slain,
His soul was once an offering made
    For every soul of man.

Awake from guilty nature's sleep,
    And Christ shall give you light,
Cast all your sins into the deep,
    And wash the Ethiop white.

With me, your chief, ye then shall know,
    Shall feel your sins forgiven;
Anticipate your heaven below,
    And own that love is heaven.

1740

Come, Sinners, to the Gospel Feast

Come, sinners, to the gospel feast;
Let every soul be Jesu's guest;
Ye need not one be left behind,

For God hath bidden all mankind.
Sent by my Lord, on you I call:
The invitation is to all:
Come all the world; come, sinner, thou!
All things in Christ are ready now.

Come, all ye souls by sin oppressed,
Ye restless wanderers after rest;
Ye poor, and maimed, and halt, and blind,
In Christ a hearty welcome find.

Come, and partake the gospel feast,
Be saved from sin, in Jesus rest;
Oh, taste the goodness of your God,
And eat his flesh, and drink his blood.

Ye vagrant souls, on you I call
(Oh, that my voice could reach you all!):
Ye all are freely justified,
Ye all may live—for Christ hath died.

My message as from God receive:
Ye all may come to Christ, and live.
Oh, let his love your hearts constrain,
Nor suffer him to die in vain!

His love is mighty to compel;
His conqu'ring love consent to feel,
Yield to his love's resistless power,
And fight against your God no more.

See him set forth before your eyes,
That precious, bleeding sacrifice!
His offered benefits embrace,
And freely now be saved by grace!

This is the time: no more delay!
This is the acceptable day;
Come in, this moment, at his call,
And live for him who died for all!

1747

Christian Life

Happy the Man That Finds the Grace

Happy the man that finds the grace,
The blessing of God's chosen race,
The wisdom coming from above,
The faith that sweetly works by love.

Happy beyond description he
Who knows, the Savior died for me,
The gift unspeakable obtains,
And heavenly understanding gains.

Wisdom divine! Who tells the price
Of wisdom's costly merchandise?
Wisdom to silver we prefer,
And gold is dross compared to her.

Her hands are filled with length of days,
True riches, and immortal praise:
Riches of Christ on all bestowed,
And honor, that descends from God.

To purest joys she all invites,
Chaste, holy, spiritual delights;
Her ways are ways of pleasantness,
And all her flowery paths are peace.

Happy the man who wisdom gains;
Thrice happy who his guest retains;

He owns, and shall forever own,
Wisdom, and Christ, and heaven are one.

1747

Let Earth and Heaven Agree

Let earth and heaven agree,
Angels and men be joined,
To celebrate with me
The Savior of mankind;
T'adore the all-atoning Lamb,
And bless the sound of Jesu's name.

Jesus, transporting sound!
The joy of earth and heaven!
No other help is found,
No other name is given
By which we can salvation have:
But Jesus came the world to save.

Jesus, harmonious name!
It charms the hosts above;
They evermore proclaim,
And wonder at his love;
'Tis all their happiness to gaze,
'Tis heaven to see our Jesu's face.

His name the sinner hears,
And is from sin set free;
'Tis music in his ears,

'Tis life and victory;
New songs do now his lips employ,
And dances his glad heart for joy.

Stung by the scorpion sin
My poor expiring soul
The balmy sound drinks in,
And is at once made whole.
See there my Lord upon the tree!
I hear, I feel, he died for me.

O unexampled love!
O all-redeeming grace!
How swiftly didst thou move
To save a fallen race!
What shall I do to make it known
What thou for all mankind hast done!

Oh, for a trumpet-voice
On all the world to call,
To bid their hearts rejoice
In him who died for all!
For all my Lord was crucified,
For all, for all my Savior died!

To serve thy blessed will,
Thy dying love to praise,
Thy counsel to fulfill,
And minister thy grace,

Freely what I receive to give,
The life of heaven on earth I live.

1742

Author of Faith, Eternal Word

Author of faith, eternal Word,
    Whose spirit breathes the active flame,
Faith, like its finisher and Lord,
    Today as yesterday the same;

To thee our humble hearts aspire,
    And ask the gift unspeakable;
Increase in us the kindled fire,
    In us the work of faith fulfill.

By faith we know thee strong to save
    (Save us, a present Savior thou!)
Whate'er we hope, by faith we have,
    Future and past subsisting now.

To him that in thy name believes
    Eternal life with thee is given;
Into himself he all receives—
    Pardon, and holiness, and heaven.

The things unknown to feeble sense,
    Unseen by reason's glimmering ray,
With strong commanding evidence
    Their heavenly origin display.

Faith lends its realizing light,
    The clouds disperse, the shadows fly;
Th'Invisible appears in sight,
    And God is seen by mortal eye.

            1740

Jesu, If Still the Same Thou Art

Jesu, if still the same thou art,
    If all thy promises are sure,
Set up thy kingdom in my heart,
    And make me rich, for I am poor:
To me be all thy treasures given,
The kingdom of an inward heaven.

Thou hast pronounced the mourners blest,
    And lo! for thee I ever mourn.
I cannot, no, I will not rest
    Till thou my only rest return;
Till thou, the Prince of peace, appear,
And I receive the Comforter.

Where is the blessedness bestowed
    On all that hunger after thee?I hunger now,
I thirst for God!
    See the poor fainting sinner, see,
And satisfy with endless peace,
And fill me with thy righteousness.

Ah, Lord!—if thou art in that sigh,
    Then hear thyself within me pray.
Hear in my heart thy Spirit's cry,
    Mark what my laboring soul would say,
Answer the deep, unuttered groan,
And show that thou and I are one.

Shine on thy work, disperse the gloom;
    Light in thy light I then shall see.
Say to my soul, "Thy light is come,
    Glory divine is risen on thee;
Thy warfare's past, thy mourning's o'er;
Look up, for thou shalt weep no more."

Lord, I believe the promise sure,
    And trust thou wilt not long delay;
Hungry, and sorrowful, and poor,
    Upon thy word myself I stay;
Into thine hands my all resign,
And wait till all thou art is mine!

1740

Soldiers of Christ, Arise

Soldiers of Christ, arise,
And put your armor on,
Strong in the strength which God supplies
Through his eternal Son;
Strong in the Lord of hosts,
And in his mighty power,
Who in the strength of Jesus trusts
Is more than conqueror.

Stand then in his great might,
With all his strength endued,
But take to arm you for the fight
The panoply of God;
That having all things done,
And all your conflicts passed,
Ye may o'ercome through Christ alone
And stand entire at last.

Stand then against your foes
In close and firm array;
Legions of wily fiends oppose
Throughout the evil day;
But meet the sons of night,
But mock their vain design,
Armed in the arms of heavenly light,
Of righteousness divine.

Leave no unguarded place,
No weakness of the soul;
Take every virtue, every grace,
And fortify the whole;
Indissolubly joined,
To battle all proceed,
But arm yourselves with all the mind
That was in Christ your head.

1749

Be It My Only Wisdom Here

Be it my only wisdom here,
To serve the Lord with filial fear,
With loving gratitude;
Superior sense may I display
By shunning every evil way,
And walking in the good.

Oh, may I still from sin depart;
A wise and understanding heart,
Jesus, to me be given!
And let me through thy Spirit know
To glorify my God below,
And find my way to heaven.

1762

Servant of All, to Toil for Man

Servant of all, to toil for man
    Thou didst not, Lord, refuse;
Thy Majesty did not disdain
    To be employed for us!

Thy bright example I pursue,
    To thee in all things rise;
And all I think, or speak, or do,
    Is one great sacrifice.

Careless through outward cares I go,
    From all distraction free;
My hands are but engaged below—
    My heart is still with thee.
               1739

Forth in Thy Name, O Lord, I Go

Forth in thy name, O Lord, I go,
    My daily labor to pursue,
Thee, only thee resolved to know
    In all I think, or speak, or do.

The task thy wisdom has assigned
    Oh, let me cheerfully fulfill,
In all my works thy presence find,
    And prove thy acceptable will.

Thee may I set at my right hand
    Whose eyes my inmost substance see,
And labor on at thy command,
    And offer all my works to thee.

Give me to bear thy easy yoke,
    And every moment watch and pray,
And still to things eternal look,
    And hasten to thy glorious day;

For thee delightfully employ
    Whate'er thy bounteous grace hath given,
And run my course with even joy,
    And closely walk with thee to heaven.

1749

O Thou Who Camest from Above

O thou who camest from above
    The pure celestial fire t'impart,
Kindle a flame of sacred love
    On the mean altar of my heart!

There let it for thy glory burn
    With inextinguishable blaze,
And trembling to its source return
    In humble love, and fervent praise.

Jesu, confirm my heart's desire
    To work, and speak, and think for thee;

Still let me guard the holy fire,
        And still stir up thy gift in me;

Ready for all thy perfect will,
        My acts of faith and love repeat,
Till death thy endless mercies seal
        And make the sacrifice complete.

/ 1762

When Quiet in My House I Sit

When quiet in my house I sit,
        Thy book be my companion still;
My joy thy sayings to repeat,
        Talk o'er the records of thy will,
And search the oracles divine
Till every heartfelt word be mine.

Oh, may the gracious words divine
        Subject of all my converse be;
So will the Lord his follower join,
        And walk and talk himself with me;
So shall my heart his presence prove,
And burn with everlasting love.

Oft as I lay me down to rest,
        Oh, may the reconciling word
Sweetly compose my weary breast,
        While on the bosom of my Lord,

I sink in blissful dreams away
And visions of eternal day.

Rising to sing my Savior's praise,
 Thee may I publish all day long,
And let thy precious word of grace
 Flow from my heart, and fill my tongue,
Fill all my life with purest love,
And join me to thy church above.

1762

Thou, Jesu, Thou My Breast Inspire

Thou, Jesu, thou my breast inspire,
And touch my lips with hallowed fire,
 And loose a stammering infant's tongue;
Prepare the vessel of thy grace,
Adorn me with the robes of praise,
 And mercy shall be all my song:
Mercy for all who know not God,
Mercy for all in Jesu's blood,
 Mercy, that earth and heaven transcends;
Love, that o'erwhelms the saints in light,
The length, and breadth, and depth, and height
 Of love divine, which never ends.

A faithful witness of thy grace,
Well may I fill th'allotted space,
 And answer all thy great design;

Walk in the works by thee prepared,
And find annexed the vast reward,
   The crown of righteousness divine.
When I have lived to thee alone,
Pronounce the welcome word, "Well done!"
   And let me take my place above,
Enter into my Master's joy,
And all eternity employ
   In praise, and ecstasy, and love.

          1749

Prayer

Spirit of Faith, Come Down

Spirit of faith, come down,
Reveal the things of God,
And make to us the Godhead known,
And witness with the blood:
'Tis thine the blood t'apply,
And give us eyes to see,
Who did for every sinner die
Hath surely died for me.

No man can truly say
That Jesus is the Lord
Unless thou take the veil away,
And breathe the living word;
Then, only then we feel
Our interest in his blood,
And cry with joy unspeakable,
Thou art my Lord, my God!

Oh, that the world might know
The all-atoning Lamb!
Spirit of faith, descend, and show
The virtue of his name;
The grace which all may find,
The saving power impart,
And testify to all mankind,
And speak in every heart!

Inspire the living faith
    (Which whosoe'er receives,
The witness in himself he hath,
    And consciously believes),
    The faith that conquers all,
    And doth the mountain move,
And saves whoe'er on Jesus call,
    And perfects them in love.

                    1746

Come, Holy Ghost, Our Hearts Inspire

Come, Holy Ghost, our hearts inspire,
    Let us thine influence prove,
Source of the old prophetic fire,
    Fountain of life and love.

Come, Holy Ghost (for moved by thee
    The prophets wrote and spoke);
Unlock the truth, thyself the key,
    Unseal the sacred book.

Expand thy wings, celestial dove,
    Brood o'er our nature's night;
On our disordered spirits move,
    And let there now be light.

God through himself we then shall know,
    If thou within us shine;

And sound, with all thy saints below,
    The depths of love divine.

1740

Jesu, My Strength, My Hope

    Jesu, my strength, my hope,
    On thee I cast my care,
With humble confidence look up,
    And know thou hear'st my prayer.
    Give me on thee to wait,
    Till I can all things do,
On thee almighty to create,
    Almighty to renew.

    I want a sober mind,
    A self-renouncing will
That tramples down and casts behind
    The baits of pleasing ill:
    A soul inured to pain,
    To hardship, grief, and loss,
Bold to take up, firm to sustain
    The consecrated cross.

    I want a godly fear,
    A quick-discerning eye,
That looks to thee when sin is near
    And sees the tempter fly;
    A spirit still prepared

And armed with jealous care,
    Forever standing on its guard,
        And watching unto prayer.

        I want a heart to pray,
            To pray and never cease,
    Never to murmur at thy stay,
        Or wish my sufferings less;
        This blessing above all,
        Always to pray I want,
    Out of the deep on thee to call,
        And never, never faint.

        I want a true regard,
            A single, steady aim,
    Unmoved by threat'ning or reward,
        To thee and thy great name;
        A jealous, just concern
        For thine immortal praise;
    A pure desire that all may learn
        And glorify thy grace.

        I rest upon thy Word,
            The promise is for me;
    My succor, and salvation, Lord,
        Shall surely come from thee.
        But let me still abide,
        Nor from thy hope remove,

Till thou my patient spirit guide
　Into thy perfect love.
　　　　　　　1742

Lord, That I May Learn of Thee

Lord, that I may learn of thee,
Give me true simplicity;
Wean my soul, and keep it low,
Willing thee alone to know.

Let me cast my reeds aside,
All that feeds my knowing pride,
Not to man, but God submit,
Lay my reasonings at thy feet.

Of my boasted wisdom spoiled,
Docile, helpless as a child,
Only seeing in thy light,
Only walking in thy might.

Then infuse the teaching grace,
Spirit of truth and righteousness;
Knowledge, love divine impart,
Life eternal to my heart.
　　　　　　　1762

Let Us Join ('Tis God Commands)

Let us join ('tis God commands),
Let us join our hearts and hands;
Help to gain our calling's hope,
Build we each the other up.
God his blessing shall dispense,
God shall crown his ordinance,
Meet in his appointed ways,
Nourish us with social grace.

Let us then as brethren love,
Faithfully his gifts improve,
Carry on the earnest strife,
Walk in holiness of life.
Still forget the things behind,
Follow Christ in heart and mind;
Toward the mark unwearied press,
Seize the crown of righteousness!

Plead we thus for faith alone,
Faith which by our works is shown;
God it is who justifies,
Only faith the grace applies,
Active faith that lives within,
Conquers earth, and hell, and sin,
Sanctifies, and makes us whole,
Forms the Savior in the soul.

Let us for this faith contend,
Sure salvation is its end;
Heaven already is begun,
Everlasting life is won.
Only let us persevere
Till we see our Lord appear;
Never from the rock remove,
Saved by faith which works by love.

1740

Rejoicing

Oft I in My Heart Have Said

Oft I in my heart have said,
    Who shall ascend on high?
Mount to Christ my glorious head,
    And bring him from the sky?
Borne on contemplation's wing,
    Surely I should find him there,
Where the angels praise their King,
    And gain the morning star.

Oft I in my heart have said,
    Who to the deep shall stoop?
Sink with Christ among the dead,
    From thence to bring him up?
Could I but my heart prepare,
    By unfeigned humility,
Christ would quickly enter there,
    And ever dwell with me.

But the righteousness of faith
    Hath taught me better things:
"Inward turn thine eyes" (it saith,
    While Christ to me it brings),
"Christ is ready to impart

Life to all for life who sigh;
In thy mouth, and in thy heart,
The word is ever nigh."

1742

And Can It Be That I Should Gain

And can it be that I should gain
An interest in the Savior's blood?
Died he for me, who caused his pain?
For me? Who him to death pursued?
Amazing love! How can it be
That thou, my God, shouldst die for me?

'Tis myst'ry all: th'Immortal dies!
Who can explore his strange design?
In vain the firstborn seraph tries
To sound the depths of love divine.
'Tis mercy all! Let earth adore!
Let angel minds inquire no more.

He left his Father's throne above
(So free, so infinite his grace!),
Emptied himself of all but love,
And bled for Adam's helpless race.
'Tis mercy all, immense and free,
For, O my God, it found out me!

Long my imprisoned spirit lay,
    Fast bound in sin and nature's night.
Thine eye diffused a quick'ning ray;
    I woke; the dungeon flamed with light.
My chains fell off, my heart was free,
I rose, went forth, and followed thee.

No condemnation now I dread,
    Jesus, and all in him, is mine.
Alive in him, my living head,
    And clothed in righteousness divine,

Bold I approach th'eternal throne,
And claim the crown, through Christ my own.

1739

Jesus, Thou Soul of All Our Joys

Jesus, thou soul of all our joys,
For whom we now lift up our voice,
    And all our strength exert,
Vouchsafe the grace we humbly claim,
Compose into a thankful frame,
    And tune thy people's heart.

While in the heavenly work we join,
Thy glory be our sole design,
    Thy glory, not our own;
Still let us keep our end in view,

And still the pleasing task pursue,
  To please our God alone.

The secret pride, the subtle sin,
Oh, let it never more steal in,
  T'offend thy glorious eyes,
To desecrate our hallowed strain,
And make our solemn service vain,
  And mar our sacrifice.

To magnify thy awful name,
To spread the honors of the Lamb,
  Let us our voices raise;
Our souls and bodies' powers unite,
Regardless of our own delight,
  And dead to human praise.

Still let us on our guard be found,
And watch against the power of sound
  With sacred jealousy;
Lest haply sense should damp our zeal,
And music's charms bewitch and steal
  Our heart away from thee.

That hurrying strife far off remove,
That noisy burst of selfish love
  Which swells the formal song;
The joy from out our heart arise,
And speak, and sparkle in our eyes,
  And vibrate on our tongue.

Then let us praise our common Lord,
And sweetly join with one accord
    Thy goodness to proclaim;
Jesus, thyself in us reveal,
And all our faculties shall feel
    Thy harmonizing name.

With calmly reverential joy,
Oh, let us all our lives employ
    In setting forth thy love;
And raise in death our triumph higher,
And sing, with all the heavenly choir,
    That endless song above.

                    1749

My God, I Am Thine; What a Comfort Divine

My God, I am thine; what a comfort divine,
What a blessing to know that my Jesus is mine!
In the heavenly Lamb thrice happy I am,
And my heart it doth dance at the sound of his
name.

True pleasures abound in the rapturous sound;
And whoever hath found it hath paradise found.
My Jesus to know, and feel his blood flow,
'Tis life everlasting, 'tis heaven below!

Yet onward I haste to the heavenly feast;
That, that is the fullness, but this is the taste;

And this I shall prove, till with joy I remove
To the heaven of heavens in Jesus' love.

1749

Thou Hidden Source of Calm Repose

Thou hidden source of calm repose,
    Thou all-sufficient love divine,
My help and refuge from my foes,
    Secure I am, if thou art mine:
And lo! from sin, and grief, and shame,
I hide me, Jesus, in thy name.

Thy mighty name salvation is,
    And keeps my happy soul above;
Comfort it brings, and power, and peace,
    And joy, and everlasting love:
To me with thy dear name are given
Pardon, and holiness, and heaven.

Jesu, my all in all thou art,
    My rest in toil, my ease in pain;
The med'cine of my broken heart,
    In war my peace, in loss my gain;
My smile beneath the tyrant's frown,
In shame my glory and my crown.

In want my plentiful supply,
    In weakness my almighty power;
In bonds my perfect liberty,

My light in Satan's darkest hour;
In grief my joy unspeakable,
My life in death, my heaven in hell.

1749

Talk with Us, Lord, Thyself Reveal

Talk with us, Lord, thyself reveal,
    While here o'er earth we rove;
Speak to our hearts, and let us feel
    The kindling of thy love.

With thee conversing we forget
    All time, and toil, and care:
Labor is rest, and pain is sweet
    If thou, my God, art here.

Here then, my God, vouchsafe to stay,
    And bid my heart rejoice;
My bounding heart shall own thy sway,
    And echo to thy voice.

Thou callest me to seek thy face—
    'Tis all I wish to seek;
To attend the whispers of thy grace,
    And hear thee inly speak.

Let this my every hour employ,
    Till I thy glory see,

Enter into my Master's joy,
    And find my heaven in thee.
            1740

Meet and Right It Is to Sing

Meet and right it is to sing,
    In every time and place,
Glory to our heavenly King,
    The God of truth and grace.

Join we then with sweet accord,
    All in one thanksgiving join:
Holy, holy, holy, Lord,
    Eternal praise be thine!

Thee the firstborn sons of light,
    In choral symphonies,
Praise by day, day without night,
    And never, never cease;
Angels and archangels all
    Praise the mystic Three in One,
Sing, and stop, and gaze, and fall
    O'erwhelmed before thy throne.

Vying with that happy choir
    Who chant thy praise above,
We on eagles' wings aspire,

The wings of faith and love;
Thee they sing with glory crowned,
    We extol the slaughtered Lamb;
Lower if our voices sound
    Our subject is the same.

Father, God, thy love we praise
    Which gave thy Son to die;
Jesus, full of truth and grace,
    Alike we glorify;
Spirit, Comforter divine,
    Praise by all to thee be given,
Till we in full chorus join,
    And earth is turned to heaven.

                    1749

Hail, Father, Son, and Holy Ghost

Hail, Father, Son, and Holy Ghost,
    One God in Persons Three;
Of thee we make our joyful boast,
    Our songs we make of thee.

Thou neither canst be felt or seen;
    Thou art a spirit pure;
Thou from eternity hast been,
    And always shalt endure.

Present alike in every place,
    Thy Godhead we adore;

Beyond the bounds of time and space
    Thou dwell'st for evermore.

In wisdom infinite thou art,
    Thine eye doth all things see,
And every thought of every heart
    Is fully known to thee.

Whate'er thou wilt in earth below
    Thou dost in heaven above;
But chiefly we rejoice to know
    Th'Almighty God of love.

Thou lov'st whate'er thy hands have made;
    Thy goodness we rehearse,
In shining characters displayed
    Throughout our universe.

Mercy, with love, and endless grace
    O'er all thy works doth reign;
But mostly thou delight'st to bless
    Thy favorite creature, man.

Wherefore let every creature give
    To thee the praise designed;
But chiefly, Lord, the thanks receive,
    The hearts of all mankind.

1763

Suffering and Death

Thee, Jesus, Full of Truth and Grace

Thee, Jesus, full of truth and grace,
    Thee, Savior, we adore;
Thee in affliction's furnace praise,
    And magnify thy power.

Thy power in human weakness shown
    Shall make us all entire;
We now thy guardian presence own,
    And walk unburnt in fire.

Thee, Son of man, by faith we see,
    And glory in our Guide,
Surrounded and upheld by thee,
    The fiery test abide.

The fire our graces shall refine
    Till, molded from above,
We bear the character divine,
    The stamp of perfect love.

        1749

Glory Be to God on High

Glory be to God on high,
God in whom we live and die,

God, who guides us by his love,
Takes us to his throne above!
Angels that surround his throne
Sing the wonders he hath done,
Shout, while we on earth reply,
Glory be to God on high!

God of everlasting grace,
Worthy thou of endless praise,
Thou hast all thy blessings shed
On the living and the dead:
Thou wast here their sure defense,
Thou hast borne their spirits hence,
Worthy thou of endless praise,
God of everlasting grace.

Thanks be all ascribed to thee,
Blessing, power, and majesty,
Thee, by whose almighty name
They their latest foe o'ercame;
Thou the victory hast won,
Saved them by thy grace alone,
Caught them up thy face to see,
Thanks be all ascribed to thee!

Happy in thy glorious love,
We shall from the vale remove,
Glad partakers of our hope,

We shall soon be taken up;
Meet again our heavenly friends,
Blest with bliss that never ends,
Joined to all thy hosts above,
Happy in thy glorious love!

1747

Oh, for a Heart to Praise My God

Oh, for a heart to praise my God,
    A heart from sin set free!
A heart that always feels thy blood,
    So freely spilt for me!

A heart resigned, submissive, meek,
    My great Redeemer's throne,
Where only Christ is heard to speak,
    Where Jesus reigns alone.

Oh! for a lowly, contrite heart,
    Believing, true, and clean,
Which neither life nor death can part
    From him that dwells within.

A heart in every thought renewed,
    And full of love divine,
Perfect, and right, and pure, and good—
    A copy, Lord, of thine!

Thy tender heart is still the same,
    And melts at human woe;
Jesu, for thee distressed I am—
    I want thy love to know.

My heart, thou know'st, can never rest
    Till thou create my peace

Till, of my Eden repossessed,
    From every sin I cease.

Fruit of thy gracious lips, on me
    Bestow that peace unknown,
The hidden manna, and the tree
    Of life, and the white stone.

Thy nature, gracious Lord, impart;
    Come quickly from above;
Write thy new name upon my heart,
    Thy new, best name of love!
1742

Jesu, Shall I Never Be

Jesu, shall I never be
Firmly grounded upon thee?
Never by thy work abide,
Never in thy wounds reside?

Oh, how wavering is my mind,
Tossed about with every wind!
Oh, how quickly doth my heart
From the living God depart!

Jesu, let my nature feel
Thou art God unchangeable;
Jah, Jehovah, great I AM,
Speak into my soul thy name.

Grant that every moment I
May believe, and feel thee nigh,
Steadfastly behold thy face,
'Stablished with abiding grace.

Plant and root, and fix in me
All the mind that was in thee;
Settled peace I then shall find—
Jesu's is a quiet mind.

Anger I no more shall feel,
Always even, always still;
Meekly on my God reclined—
Jesu's is a gentle mind.

I shall suffer, and fulfill
All my Father's gracious will,
Be in all alike resigned—
Jesu's is a patient mind.

When 'tis deeply rooted here
Perfect love shall cast out fear;
Fear doth servile spirits bind—
Jesu's is a noble mind.

When I feel it fixed within
I shall have no power to sin;
How shall sin an entrance find?
Jesu's is a spotless mind.

I shall nothing know beside
Jesus, and him crucified;
I shall all to him be joined—
Jesu's is a loving mind.

I shall triumph evermore,
Gratefully my God adore,
God so good, so true, so kind—
Jesu's is a thankful mind.

Lowly, loving, meek, and pure,
I shall to the end endure;
Be no more to sin inclined—
Jesu's is a constant mind.

I shall fully be restored
To the image of my Lord,
Witnessing to all mankind
Jesu's is a perfect mind.

                    1742

Jesus, the Divine Gift I Know

Jesus, the gift divine I know,
    The gift divine I ask of thee;
That living water now bestow,
    Thy Spirit and thyself on me.
Thou, Lord, of life the fountain art:
Now let me find thee in my heart!

Thee let me drink, and thirst no more
    For drops of finite happiness;
Spring up, O well, in heavenly power,
    In streams of pure, perennial peace,
In peace, that none can take away,
In joy, which shall forever stay.

Father, on me the grace bestow,
    Unblameable before thy sight,
Whence all the streams of mercy flow;
    Mercy, thy own supreme delight,
To me, for Jesu's sake impart,
And plant thy nature in my heart.

Thy mind throughout my life be shown,
    While listening to the wretch's cry,
The widow's and the orphan's groan,
    On mercy's wings I swiftly fly
The poor and helpless to relieve,
My life, my all for them to give.

Thus may I show thy Spirit within,
    Which purges me from every stain;
Unspotted from the world and sin
    My faith's integrity maintain,
The truth of my religion prove
By perfect purity and love.

1762

Love Divine, All Loves Excelling

Love divine, all loves excelling,
    Joy of heaven, to earth come down,
Fix in us thy humble dwelling,
    All thy faithful mercies crown!
Jesu, thou art all compassion,
    Pure, unbounded love thou art;
Visit us with thy salvation!
    Enter every trembling heart.

Come, almighty to deliver,
    Let us all thy grace receive;
Suddenly return, and never,
    Never more thy temples leave.
Thee we would be always blessing,
    Serve thee as thy hosts above,
Pray, and praise thee without ceasing,
    Glory in thy perfect love.

Finish then thy new creation,
    Pure and spotless let us be;
Let us see thy great salvation
    Perfectly restored in thee;
Changed from glory into glory,
    Till in heaven we take our place,
Till we cast our crowns before thee,
    Lost in wonder, love, and praise.

1747

God and Doctrine

Lo! He Comes with Clouds Descending

Lo! He comes with clouds descending,
    Once for favored sinners slain;
Thousand thousand saints attending,
    Swell the triumph of his train:
    Hallelujah!
    God appears on earth to reign.

Every eye shall now behold him
    Robed in dreadful majesty;
Those who set at naught and sold him,
    Pierced and nailed him to the tree,
    Deeply wailing,
    Shall the true Messiah see.

The dear tokens of his passion
    Still his dazzling body bears;
Cause of endless exultation
    To his ransomed worshipers;
    With what rapture
    Gaze we on those glorious scars!

Yea, Amen! let all adore thee,
    High on thy eternal throne;
Savior, take the power and glory
    Claim the kingdom for thine own;

Jah, Jehovah,
Everlasting God, come down!
1758

Jesu, Lover of My Soul

Jesu, Lover of my soul,
    Let me to thy bosom fly,
While the nearer waters roll,
    While the tempest still is high:
Hide me, O my Savior, hide,
    Till the storm of life be past!
Safe into the haven guide,
    Oh, receive my soul at last!

Other refuge have I none,
    Hangs my helpless soul on thee;
Leave, ah! leave me not alone,
    Still support and comfort me:
All my trust on thee is stayed,
    All my help from thee I bring;
Cover my defenseless head
    With the shadow of thy wing.

Thou, O Christ, art all I want
    More than all in thee I find!
Raise the fallen, cheer the faint,
    Heal the sick, and lead the blind;
Just and holy is thy name,

I am all unrighteousness;
    False and full of sin I am,
        Thou art full of truth and grace.

Plenteous grace with thee is found,
        Grace to cover all my sin,
Let the healing streams abound;
        Make and keep me pure within:
Thou of life the fountain art,
        Freely let me take of thee,
Spring thou up within my heart,
        Rise to all eternity.

                    1740

Jesus, the All-Restoring Word

Jesus, the all-restoring Word,
        My fallen spirit's hope,
After thy lovely likeness, Lord,
        Ah, when shall I wake up?

Thou, O my God, thou only art
        The Life, the Truth, the Way;
Quicken my soul, instruct my heart,
        My sinking footsteps stay.

Of all thou hast in earth below,
        In heaven above, to give,
Give me thy only love to know,
        In thee to walk and live.

Fill me with all the life of love;
        In mystic union join
Me to thyself, and let me prove
        The fellowship divine.

Open the intercourse between
        My longing soul and thee,
Never to be broke off again
        To all eternity.

                    1740

Hark How All the Welkin Rings

Hark how all the welkin rings,
"Glory to the King of kings,
Peace on earth, and mercy mild,
God and sinners reconciled!"

Joyful, all ye nations, rise,
Join the triumph of the skies;
Universal Nature, say,
"Christ the Lord is born today!"

Christ, by highest heaven adored,
Christ, the everlasting Lord,
Late in time behold him come,
Offspring of a virgin's womb.

Veil'd in flesh, the Godhead see,
Hail th'Incarnate Deity!

Pleased as man with men t'appear
Jesus, our *Immanuel* here!

Hail the heavenly Prince of Peace!
Hail the Sun of Righteousness!
Light and life to all he brings,
Risen with healing in his wings.

Mild he lays his glory by,
Born—that man no more may die,
Born—to raise the sons of earth,
Born—to give them second birth.

Come, Desire of Nations, come
Fix in us thy humble home;
Rise, the woman's conquering Seed,
Bruise in us the serpent's head.

Now display thy saving power,
Ruin'd nature now restore;
Now in mystic union join
Thine to ours, and ours to thine.

Adam's likeness, Lord, efface
Stamp thy image in its place;
Second *Adam* from above,
Reinstate us in Thy love.

Let us thee, though lost, regain,
Thee, the Life, the Inner Man:

Oh! to all Thyself impart,
Form'd in each believing heart.

1739

Come, Thou Long-Expected Jesus

Come, thou long-expected Jesus,
    Born to set thy people free,
From our fears and sins release us,
    Let us find our rest in thee.
Israel's strength and consolation,
    Hope of all the earth thou art;
Dear Desire of every nation,
    Joy of every longing heart.

Born thy people to deliver,
    Born a child and yet a king,
Born to reign in us forever,
    Now thy gracious kingdom bring:
By thine own eternal Spirit
    Rule in all our hearts alone;
By thine all-sufficient merit
    Raise us to thy glorious throne.

1746

Christ the Lord Is Risen Today

"Christ the Lord is risen today,"
Sons of men and angels say!
Raise your joys and triumphs high:
Sing, ye heavens; thou earth reply.

Love's redeeming work is done;
Fought the fight, the battle won:
Lo! the sun's eclipse is o'er,
Lo! he sets in blood no more!

Vain the stone, the watch, the seal,
Christ hath burst the gates of hell:
Death in vain forbids his rise,
Christ hath opened Paradise.

Lives again our glorious King!
Where, O death, is now thy sting!
Once he died our souls to save;
Where's thy victory, boasting grave!

Soar we now where Christ hath led,
Following our exalted Head:
Made like him, like him we rise,
Ours the cross, the grave, the skies.

King of glory! Soul of bliss!
Everlasting life is this,
Thee to know, thy power to prove,
Thus to sing, and thus to love.

1739

Father, Whose Everlasting Love

Father, whose everlasting love
    Thy only Son for sinners gave,
Whose grace to all did freely move,
    And sent him down a world to save;

Help us thy mercy to extol,
    Immense, unfathom'd, unconfined;
To praise the Lamb who died for all,
    The general Savior of mankind.

Thy undistinguishing regard
    Was cast on Adam's fallen race;
For all thou hast in Christ prepared
    Sufficient, sovereign, saving grace.

Jesus hath said, we all shall hope,
    Preventing grace for all is free:
"And I, if I be lifted up,
    I will draw all men unto Me."

What soul those drawings never knew?
    With whom hath not thy Spirit strove?
We all must own that God is true,
    We all may feel that God is love.

O all ye ends of earth, behold
    The bleeding, all-atoning Lamb!
Look unto him for sinners sold,
    Look and be saved through Jesu's name.

Behold the Lamb of God, who takes
    The sins of all the world away!
His pity no exception makes;
    But all that will receive him, may.

A world he suffer'd to redeem;
    For all he hath th'atonement made:
For those that will not come to him
    The ransom of his life was paid.

          1741

Morning Hymn

Christ, Whose Glory Fills the Skies

Christ, whose glory fills the skies,
    Christ, the true, the only Light,
Sun of righteousness, arise,
    Triumph o'er the shades of night;
Day-spring from on high, be near;
Day-star, in my heart appear!

Dark and cheerless is the morn,
    Unaccompanied by thee:
Joyless is the day's return,
    Till thy mercy's beams I see:
Till thou inward light impart,
Glad my eyes, and warm my heart.

Visit then this soul of mine,
    Pierce the gloom of sin and grief;
Fill me, Radiancy Divine!
    Scatter all my unbelief:
More and more thyself display,
Shining to the perfect day!

1740

ABOUT THE EDITOR

HarperCollins Spiritual Classics Series Editor Emilie Griffin has long been interested in the classics of the devotional life. She has written a number of books on spiritual formation and transformation, including *Clinging: The Experience of Prayer* and *Wilderness Time: A Guide to Spiritual Retreat*. With Richard J. Foster she coedited *Spiritual Classics: Selected Readings on the Twelve Spiritual Disciplines*. Her latest book is *Wonderful and Dark Is this Road: Discovering the Mystic Path*. She is a board member of Renovaré and leads retreats and workshops throughout the United States. She and her husband William live in Alexandria, Louisiana.

THE CLASSICS OF **WESTERN SPIRITUALITY**
A LIBRARY OF THE GREAT SPIRITUAL MASTERS

These volumes contain original writings of universally acknowledged teachers within the Catholic, Protestant, Eastern Orthodox, Jewish, Islamic, and American Indian traditions.

The Classics of Western Spirituality unquestionably provide the most in-depth, comprehensive, and accessible panorama of Western mysticism ever attempted. From the outset, the Classics has insisted on the highest standards for these volumes, including new translations from the original languages, and helpful introductions and other aids by internationally recognized scholars and religious thinkers, designed to help the modern reader to come to a better appreciation of these works that have nourished the three monotheistic faiths for centuries.

The Cloud of Unknowing	*Teresa of Avila*	*John of the Cross*	*John and Charles Wesley*
Edited and Introduced	Edited and Introduced	Edited and Introduced	Edited and Introduced
by James Walsh	by Kieran Kavanaugh, O.C.D.	by Kieran Kavanaugh, O.C.D.	by Frank Whaling
0-8091-2332-0 $22.95	0-8091-2254-5 $22.95	0-8091-2839-X $21.95	0-8091-2368-1 $26.95

For more information on the
CLASSICS OF WESTERN SPIRITUALITY, **contact Paulist Press**
(800) 218-1903 • **www.paulistpress.com**